Cutting Through Despair

Dare to Hope

Kathy Brasby

Zao Productions LLC

Copyright © 2022 by Kathy Brasby

All rights reserved.

No portion of this book may be reproduced in any form without written permission from the publisher or author, except as permitted by U.S. copyright law.

For Matt
1955-2022
To my number-one cheerleader. He wasn't a writer – even much of a reader – but he read every completed chapter in this book and gave me serious feedback. I miss him more than I can say.

Contents

Introduction	VII
Naomi	1
Hannah	17
Daniel's Journey	31
Grasping At Crumbs	47
The Earthquake	61
The Singer	75
The Money Chapter	91
Mechanics	105
Defeating The Dragon	119
The Wall	136
Leslie's Story	153
Zoe's Help	169
The Final Chapter	185
Appendix I: The Scroll	201
Appendix II: Bible Verses About Hope	219
About the Author	223

Introduction

"The continual looking forward to the eternal world is not a form of escapism or wishful thinking, but one of the things a Christian is meant to do."
—C. S. Lewis

"If we hope for what we do not see, we wait for it with patience."
—Romans 8:24

··········

Grappling with the idea of hope seemed so easy at the start. When I began research for a book about hope, my confidence in tackling this topic was in the clouds—and so, apparently, was my understanding of what hope really meant.

What was hope, anyway? I started with the dictionary. If I discovered a clear definition there, was there a need for a book on the topic? I could just send people to the dictionary and be done.

Well, that strategy flopped.

According to the *Concise Oxford English Dictionary*, hope is a feeling of expectation and desire.

But this word—hope—is like a butterfly flitting in and out of focus. You can't nail down the definition.

Oxford English Dictionary's second definition is "a cause or source of hope or grounds for hoping." Yeah, I think they don't know for sure how to define it either. Using the word *hope* to define it is admitting defeat.

Their archaic definition is "a feeling of trust." Archaic. Out of modern use?

There lies the problem. I didn't want a feel-good definition that had no connection with life. I wanted an understanding of hope that could marinate my heart and carry me forward with confidence.

Transparent moment: I am a Christian who trusts in God and in the truth of his word, the Bible. So, I am not convinced that the archaic definition of hope is useless. Only if the Bible is useless.

That's my opinion. But what do others think? How do they engage with the idea of hope?

I needed to know what others thought. So, I dialed up that time-honored method of surveying friends and relatives. I asked a question to my social media connections: What is godly hope?

My Christian friends chimed in, because they all were certain that they understood it. I think they didn't first consult a dictionary or their confidence might have been drooping a little. Their definitions were pretty good. Here are a few:

- Hope is an antidote to fear. If God's in our future, there's no reason to fear.

- No matter what happens, we are in God's hands, and he wants good for us.

- Hope is peace and confidence.

- Hope is Jesus.

- Hope is trust.

- Hope is salvation.

- Hope is believing God will do what he says he will do.

Great answers. I considered copying them into my book and typing "The end" because these people had nailed it. Or so I thought.

More on that in a minute.

I also searched the internet for books or blogs or articles about Christian hope. There are just under a billion (you think I didn't count them, don't you?) and they largely communicated this: "Here are Bible verses about hope. Now live it."

These ideas are all fine. As Christians, we long for hope. It should give us peace and joy and confidence.

Should is one of those Christian words that stubs our toe and brings us crashing down. It is the uneven step between definition and application, and we often stumble.

What does hope really look like as we journey through this life? When we live out godly hope, how do we get through coffee dumped all over the carpet? Or puppy doodoo?

Or hearing our cousin/aunt/grandma is dying? Or finding our car dented after lending it to a friend?

Or, like a friend who recently traveled hundreds of miles back to her hometown for her class reunion, to rise one morning to find all four tires and wheels stolen from her car in the night. What a welcome home.

Do we have peace and light when the refrigerator just gurgled its dying breath right after we had to replace the transmission in the car? And when we are called in for an extra shift? Or, worse, we are called in to learn our employer has laid us off.

And that doesn't even touch the horror of loss when a parent dies. Or a child. Or a close friend. Or when we get news of the terminal diagnosis of a loved one. Or a spouse leaves. Or strays.

·･･●●･●･･･

I've noticed that the memory of those on social media is about five days, but I waited a month before posting my next question.

I didn't think they'd recall their earlier answers about hope, and I don't think they did.

I asked this time: *What do you do when hardships hit you?*

The answers I got from friends were forthright. These same people who had given me clear definitions of Christian hope were now candid about their difficulties.

They were not immune to hardships.

Most found a distraction helped. Whether it was counting to ten—maybe a hundred—or screaming at the sky, they looked away from the difficulty. One young man meditated on flowing water, reminding himself of his own limited resources and considering what he could do right now in his difficult situation.

"A lot of time by the river has helped me get through a lot," he said.

Others sought music. Or pulling weeds.

Several acknowledged that their first response to a difficulty was not their best response. A deep breath helped. Reflecting. Intentionally staying calm. Even a cup of tea could help. Or asking others for input.

Some withdrew emotionally, and often physically, to a safe place. Distance often leads to over-thinking or to prayer. People seemed to lean into one or the other.

Most were honest: difficulties could tip them into gloom and even depression. They had to work out strategies to counteract that. Often, a dive into scripture or worship helped.

The honesty in these answers struck me. Do we have difficulties? Oh, yeah. Almost daily. And hardships annoy us, confuse us, steal away our yellow morning light. Instead, bruises form on our soul. We walk in darkness. Limping.

And then, as Christians, we return to the question: what is hope and what can it do for us?

We often use the word hope to mean wish or dream. Nothing is wrong with that usage until we think it applies to our interactions with God.

We're back to that dictionary conundrum again. Christian hope—godly hope—is not about wishing or dreaming. If it is, there's no confidence for us.

We might hope our bank account has enough money to cover the last debit card payment we just posted. But there's no assurance in that hope. We might hope that buckling our seat belt and taking our vitamins will keep us safe from any disease or any harm. But that's not an absolute solution and we know it.

Godly hope is vibrant. Energetic. Refreshing. And we sort of understand it. But in our English language, when a word has more than one meaning, we figure out which meaning is appropriate by the context.

That doesn't help us much with the word *hope*. If I say to you, "I hope that you have a safe trip," can you tell if I'm desiring you to have a safe trip or I'm guaranteeing a safe trip?

We assume the former because, well, I don't have the power to guarantee a safe trip.

But the trick, for Christians, is that God has that power and we know it. So, we need some help to discern what hope means when God's involved.

··········

We can use stories to help us connect definition with application, so that we have confidence in God when hardships strike. Because hardships will strike.

Stories give us muscle memory. Randy Ingermanson tells the tale of a young man, in ancient times, pressed into service by his villagers to help hunt a killer tiger. The young man had little experience hunting tigers and even less handling the spear in his hand. Untrained and frightened, he didn't want to join the other hunters.

But this tiger must be executed, or it would destroy all the goats and sheep of the village. Then the village would die. Even though he was terrified, the boy knew he must join the other hunters to protect his village.

The hunters fanned out to form a giant circle around the area where they had last heard the tiger. Thick green leaves blocked their view. As the hunters advanced toward where they thought the tiger was hiding, the boy felt sweat run down his back. Fear squeezed his body, and his heart thumped. His spear arm shook. Breaths were shallow and quick.

But he walked in unison with the others.

The hunters closed the circle and found the tiger. Its powerful orange and black body crouched close to the ground. It snarled and snapped big white teeth, its head turning from side to side. The hunters stepped closer, tightening the loop around the tiger.

The tiger searched the hunters, and its eyes settled on the boy. He was the smallest and his spear shook in his hand.

The tiger leaped toward this weakest member.

But as the tiger lunged forward, the boy remembered the stories he'd heard many times: *Face the tiger. Wait till the last possible moment to throw the spear. Kill the tiger, even if the tiger also kills you. Face the tiger.*

It was like he had done this a thousand times before. He waited, the spear damp with his sweat. He drew back the spear. The tiger came closer, its yellow eyes narrow with hate. He waited.

The tiger crashed into him, knocking him into darkness. His last memory before the darkness was shoving the spear forward. Kill or be killed.

He awoke to hear drumming and shouting in the village. A feast.

His body throbbed with the marks of the tiger's claws, but he knew the tiger was dead. He had saved the village.

Ingermanson describes the muscle memory of stories. We don't have to experience every challenge to know how to handle it when things get tough. We can learn from the experiences of others.

Not all wisdom comes from personal experience, but also comes from grasping others' stories.

In the coming chapters, we're going to examine stories of how others discovered hope as they learned from their mistakes and from their triumphs. Through stories like these, we also develop muscle memory for hope and for a future.

The dictionary offers wimpy definitions of hope, but we can uncover a powerful explanation and also a vigorous application of hope when we trust God.

The tiger didn't defeat the warrior boy because he remembered the lessons of the past. Hardships don't have to defeat us either. For the same reason.

The stories in the following chapters are gritty. Painful sometimes. Honest and transparent. We'll meet some people—modern and historic—who wrestled with harsh circumstances.

The question I asked over and over, in interviews and in studies, was this: "How did you hang on to godly hope in these difficulties?"

Why didn't these people give up on God? Or on life? Sometimes they complained and considered abandoning their faith. Some blamed God for their problems. But they hung on because they remembered God's work in the past. Muscle memory.

In a world that seems to lose the notion of hope in God, these stories provide vivid pictures depicting a future of hope.

I will reference God's work in the Old Testament history in the following chapters. If you're hazy about Old Testament history, consider checking out *The Scroll* in the appendix.

I included a *Digging Deeper* and a *Behind the Scenes* section after each story. These are optional but allow you to engage further in the issues of each story and to journal if that's your bend.

Come along and let's explore their stories.

· · · • • • • · · ·

Digging Deeper
How do you respond to Randy Ingermanson's idea that stories help us develop a kind of muscle memory that can help us with future actions?

Can you think of a story in your own life or that of a loved one that has prepared you for a difficult time?

Behind the Scenes
Randy Ingermanson aims his book, *How to Write a Dynamic Scene Using the Snowflake Method,* at writers, but his example of muscle memory fits us all. He

describes the tiger hunt in breathtaking detail in an excerpt from his website. Highly recommended even if you're not a writer.

Naomi

"Endurance is not just the ability to bear a hard thing, but to turn it into glory."
—Philip Yancey

"They arrived in Bethlehem in late spring, at the beginning of the barley harvest."
—Ruth 1:22b

··········

One thing most of us fear is hard times, even though we know they're inevitable. When they come, and we know they will, we want to scream that it isn't fair. We don't want the pain. Difficulties kick our feet out from under us and leave us lying in an emotional black hole.

So we blame. It's easy to blame God when we expect him to make us happy. Surely a loving Father doesn't want us to suffer. So we reason.

How do we go on when the future looks black? Can we rekindle hope??

2 CUTTING THROUGH DESPAIR

We can learn while in the depths of despair. What follows is the story of a woman who initially chooses bitterness but ultimately learns that it doesn't have to be her final decision.

······•·•••···

Naomi dipped the water bags into the cool spring water. Behind her, the sunrise cast oranges and yellows that pretended to promise a lovely day but would blister by mid-day. Her feet were heavy already and dirty, but Naomi carefully closed the bags. She wanted Ruth to have water for today's journey.

Ruth finished stowing their thin blankets into bags just as Naomi returned from the well. There was no food this morning, but maybe they'd find something along the road. Berries or leaves.

"Let's get started." Naomi lifted her rough sheepskin bag containing all she owned.

They both wore widows' garb. And anyone who watched the two women walk would know there were no children with them. Another humiliation.

"Is this road the same as when you and the family came to Moab?" Ruth walked beside Naomi as their thin leather sandals padded on the hard dirt road. Thin yellow grass filled the hills on each side of the road. Two thin trees in the distance poked through the grass carpe.

"The same, I suppose." Naomi didn't care. One road looked like another and their journey had been long. But she said no more. Ruth was young and had never traveled this way before.

"Did you see the bird in the acacia tree? It had a pretty song. The morning is so beautiful." Ruth looked up at the sky as though she'd find another bird singing to them. Was she about to whirl in a morning dance? Naomi glanced around. Would others be watching this?

Besides, why would a bird sing to two widows? Once, when Naomi had a husband and two sons, she was worthy of a lovely song. Those days were over.

"I wish Orpah could have seen the sunrise this morning," Ruth said. "And heard the dove. The air is so fresh in the morning. Orpah would have liked the dove's song."

"Orpah was wise to return home. There are birds in Moab, too." Naomi shifted her tiny pack to her other shoulder. It would be a long hot day and she didn't want the straps to dig any further in. "There is nothing for her in Bethlehem."

"I miss her. You know we spent a long time together. Ten years." Ruth drew in a long breath. "I miss Mahlon, too. I wish I could have given him a child."

A tear trickled down Naomi's cheek as she thought of her husband, Elimelech, and her sons, Mahlon and Kilion. How could they all die? She loved them. And Yahweh* had not kept them safe. And he hadn't kept her safe either, by letting them die. There would be no protection for her or Ruth when they got to Bethlehem. No husband. No sons. No one to provide for them.

"What will Bethlehem be like?" Ruth asked. She adjusted her head covering. The cool air of the sunrise was already melting in the heat of mid-morning. There were only a few travelers on this day, which was fine with Naomi.

Did she dare describe what they faced in Bethlehem? No point in dashing Ruth's hopes any sooner than necessary.

"I heard that famine is over. Bethlehem has crops again." Naomi had heard from a fellow traveler. She had also heard from the same messenger that Yahweh had blessed his people by giving them good crops again, but why give Yahweh much credit? They would have to beg for survival upon returning home.

And you never know what others might do. Many weren't kind.

"I'm glad Moab had crops ten years ago," Ruth said. "You came to us—you and Elimilech and Mahlon and Kilion. You wouldn't have come otherwise."

Naomi didn't speak for a time. It had been painful to leave Bethlehem, but what could they do? The famine had been a snarling wolf, forcing them out. They hadn't left Yahweh, either, but it might have been better if he had left them.

The narrow road curved around a low hill dotted with sparse pasture. Naomi could see a shepherd up high tending a few sheep. This was familiar. They were getting closer to Bethlehem.

Naomi searched the landscape for a tree or bush. It would be nice to find some shade along the way and maybe even some berries to eat.

This was their life now, looking for a few berries left by the birds. There wouldn't be much in Bethlehem for them. Mostly hunger and shame.

"Does the family have land in Bethlehem?" Ruth had skipped a few steps ahead, but she turned to Naomi, waiting.

Naomi bit back strong words. "Women can't own land," she said. "We will have nothing when we arrive. We will have to glean."

"Glean?"

"When the farmer gathers his grain, some kernels fall to the ground. Our law allows poor people to pick up those kernels for food." Naomi had seen the poor, bent over and broken, picking up a single kernel of barley. Sometimes they carefully put the grain into a small bag and sometimes they ate it immediately. A single kernel might be all they ate that day.

Ruth was silent then. Regretting her decision to join Naomi?

"You know I can't provide you with a husband in Bethlehem," Naomi said. "I am too old to bear a son. And think how long you'd wait for him to be old enough to marry you even if I could. This is all baffling. You should go back to your mother's home and your own gods. You should have children." They had discussed this before, but Naomi might as well try one more time.

Naomi knew that Ruth's mother could find her a husband. Ruth would probably be a man's second or third wife, but at least she would have some provisions. And since Yahweh was apparently angry with Naomi, a Moabite god might do a better job protecting Ruth. Naomi prepared her arguments for the next round of this discussion.

Ruth really should turn back to Moab.

Ruth looked at the far horizon, but her feet never stopped. "Don't ask me to leave you." Her voice sounded like a morning breeze. "I'm your family. My heart is with you and I won't leave you. I'm going to die in Bethlehem, where you are, when the day comes. Because of your family, I trust Yahweh, too. I'm not going back to Moab."

The dusty smells of the road thickened in Naomi's throat. So this was it, then. Ruth would join her in this widow's plight. They would be poor and hungry. And, worse, Ruth was a foreigner. What man of Bethlehem would marry a foreigner? None. Ruth was choosing a hopeless future.

They continued their journey until they came to Bethlehem. People gathered at the edge of the village to watch them approaching. Some women leaned in. "Is it really Naomi?" one said.

Naomi's skin tingled. Her eyes narrowed. She had left as Naomi, the pleasant one, the one who had a complete family, honored by the village. Now she returned alone, with nothing but shame. No husband. No sons. Empty.

She couldn't hold back any longer. "Don't call me Naomi," she told the women. Some of them had been neighbors once. They thought they knew her, but it was time to clarify things. They needed to hear what she knew: Yahweh had cursed her. She had no hope left. No future. Just the dull life of poverty, picking up dusty grains of barley until she died.

"Call me Mara, for I am bitter," she told the women. "When I left with my family, I was full. But now I am empty and alone. Yahweh did this to me. He has given me this suffering. I can't bear it."

She had returned home to die, but the filthy rag of humiliation was heavier than she expected. How could Yahweh do this to her? She pushed past the crowd.

"Is the harvest complete?" Ruth asked a woman before following Naomi.

"This is the end of the barley harvest," the woman said. "The wheat harvest is yet to come."

Ruth nodded and then scampered to catch up with Naomi. They searched until they located a small abandoned hut for shelter and settled in. They dropped their packs on the ground and Naomi scratched out an abandoned firepit. She could cook, assuming they would have anything to cook.

The next morning, Ruth announced she was going to glean.

Naomi's spine stiffened. "Do you know how dangerous that is? Harvesters might attack you. Who would protect you?" Dirty hands, leering fingers. Men reaching out toward a young widow who had no defense.

"What choice do I have?" Ruth tilted her head to one side. Pleading. "We need to eat."

She was right, of course. Naomi looked around the hut. Crumbling walls of dirt and grass. No windows. But light trickled through flaws in the roof. They had four berries from their journey yesterday, and she was tired. No food today? Her stomach growled its vote.

"Go ahead," Naomi said. Perhaps a kind landowner would watch over her. Surely there were a few.

The day was long as Naomi swept out the dirt floor of the hut and searched for dry grass to burn in a small fire in the evening. She could roast the grains that Ruth might bring home. If there was enough for her.

A fire would bring light to the corners. The breeze slipped through the cracks in the walls. This wasn't so bad now, in the spring, but what would winter bring?

Yahweh had been kind to her once. She had worshipped with Elimelech and the boys. She remembered the celebration when they had gone to Jerusalem for a Passover Festival, celebrating the barley harvest. Together they celebrated with their people, remembering how Yahweh given her people freedom. A new land.

She had never trusted the Moabite gods, even in Moab. So how had Yahweh turned on her? Stolen her family away? She had been loyal.

Her cooking pot tumbled from her pack and rolled on the ground. Like her dreams.

Naomi remembered the smell of the stews she had cooked for her family. Rabbit stew. Barley. The fragrance of coriander and mint and dill. Together, they had huddled around the fire to swallow the thick gravy. Now they were gone.

She realized the sun was fading behind the horizon. Her stomach grumbled. Would Ruth find anything? A few grains of barley would help.

Then Ruth appeared at the door of the hut, carrying a basket full of grain. A basket. Full.

Naomi's legs froze. She stared at the basket. At Ruth's face. No scratches or bruises that would have come from conflict. Ruth smiled, her face as bright as the heaping grain before her.

"What is this?" Naomi grasped the basket and set it down. It was heavy with golden grains of barley. "Where did you gather today? May Yahweh bless him." Why has she said that? She was still angry with Yahweh but she asked him to work on her behalf? Bad habit, maybe.

Ruth laughed. "It was a wonderful day. I went to the farm of Boaz. He allowed me to glean and even invited me to join his crew for lunch. See? I didn't eat all that was available. I brought some for you." She handed the roasted barley to Naomi.

The grain tamed Naomi's complaining stomach. Filled her with food—and questions. This was not what she expected in Bethlehem. What was happening here?

"Boaz is a close relative, one of our family redeemers." Naomi touched the barley in the basket. Let her finger stroke the bearded flaxen grains.

"What is a family redeemer?" Ruth settled herself on a blanket on the ground.

"We expect them to help members of the family. If a family member is in jail for failing to pay a loan, the redeemer gets the family member out of jail. Sometimes they pay a debt or buy land that is about to be sold away from the family. They help the family."

Ruth wrapped her thin arms around herself. "And Boaz is one of our family redeemers? Amazing how that happened. His was the first farm I went to."

Naomi built a fire and pushed another handful of twigs into the flames. "May Yahweh bless Boaz. He is showing kindness to my dead husband and to yours."

She watched the yellow and orange flames dance, throwing shafts of light onto the hut wall. Was Yahweh at work?

"And Boaz invited me to glean alongside his harvesters until they complete the entire harvest." Ruth scooped a few grains of barley into her mouth.

Suddenly, there was food. Protection for Ruth. Did Yahweh remember them? Naomi knew she deserved to be forgotten. She had blamed Yahweh for her losses. Why should he remember her?

· · · · • • • • · ·

Ruth continued gleaning through the barley and then the wheat harvest. When the crops were all on the threshing floor, Naomi put together a plan. It was time to think of Ruth. She needed more than this—caring for an old woman when she should care for a family.

Naomi called to Ruth, who was returning with an armful of grass and twigs for the fire. "I must find a permanent home for you. It's time for me to think about your future."

Ruth set the armful on the ground. "You're different somehow. Just this morning, I saw you singing."

Naomi laughed. "I used to sing like a bird. My voice is old and poor, but it felt good to sing." She waved her hands at Ruth. Gaining attention for the next words. "But I have a plan for you."

"For me?" Ruth sat down.

"It's time for your time of grieving to end. Get rid of the widow's garb and wash yourself. No more ashes for you. Put on your best clothes and go to Boaz." Naomi had thought through her plan well and she explained every detail. "But don't let him see you. When he falls asleep, you are to creep in and lie at his feet. Wait till he tells you what to do."

Ruth stared at her. "Isn't this risky? He's a very kind man, but what might he do? I am only a foreigner and a widow. He has status. He can do anything."

"I need to do something for your future."

"I have no dowry. No alliance to offer." Ruth fingered the folds in her robe between quivering fingers. "What if he thinks I'm offering myself as a prostitute?"

Maybe this was a crazy plan. But Naomi pushed ahead. She gathered Ruth's hands in her own to still the trembling. "It is a risk, but Boaz has shown himself to be a virtuous man. This is the only chance I have to give you some kind of future. I think he will act honorably." She held Ruth's cheeks between her hands. Lifted her face. Met her eyes. "I am responsible for you, but you have no future now. Who knows what Yahweh might do?"

Ruth stared at her for a moment and then nodded. "Yes, who knows what Yahweh might do? I will do this."

The day was filled with Ruth's preparations. A bath. A different robe. She pulled a comb through her hair and wound a new scarf over her dark hair. "What do you think?"

Naomi surveyed the new attire. "No more widow look for you. Well done."

"I almost didn't get all this completed. The sun is nearly down. I'd better go." She stepped out of the hut and then looked back at Naomi. "Ask Yahweh to help me." She disappeared into the night.

Sleep wouldn't come that night for Naomi. Dangers lay in the night for a young woman. Would Yahweh continue with his kindness? Or was this when he would slap Naomi again? Remind her of her worthlessness?

The sun had only promised morning light when Ruth returned. Naomi jumped to her feet.

"Tell me, my child. How did it go?"

"I proposed marriage," Ruth said.

Naomi stared. Well, Ruth had added spice to the plan. A lot of spice. She proposed marriage? That wasn't done. How could Ruth so misunderstand? A Jewish woman never proposed marriage.

"I had hoped he might take you as a concubine," Naomi said. "Or perhaps a servant in his household. Marriage? You proposed marriage to him?"

Ruth laughed. "I did. And I asked him to be our redeemer, to rescue both of us." Ruth pressed Naomi's hands between hers.

"Both of us? What did you ask? This is impossible."

"Not impossible. Yahweh heard our prayers. Boaz agreed to care for you, too. He is a good man."

Well, this was unexpected. Naomi only wanted to give Ruth a future. She did not know that Boaz would agree to Ruth's plan. Naomi knew she would be left alone while planning for Ruth's future. She had been prepared for that.

But the path was set. There was more business to be taken care but Boaz navigated the intricacies of the law. Soon Boaz and Ruth were married. A pregnancy followed. And then the birth of a son.

As Naomi held the infant in her arms, she remembered when Elimelech stood beside her, gently touching the newborn Mahlon's cheek. The baby cooed in her arms and Naomi felt the warmth of family love rising inside her. From Yahweh. Her face tingled.

"This son replaces your family," Ruth whispered.

And a dove sang. A song of return. A song of rescue.

A song of hope.

••••••••••

Digging Deeper:
How did Naomi's grief and loss turn into hopelessness?

What part of Naomi's story strikes home for you? Have you experienced such hopelessness or have you seen it in another?

What did you learn about God's nature in this story?

How does this help you understand hope?

Behind the scenes
The ancient system of patronage seems dense to modern Westerners, although patronage is very much alive in the world today. Patronage meant that a family member would accept responsibility for others in the family who were in hardship. This family member would provide help, expecting nothing in return except loyalty.

When Ruth proposed marriage to Boaz, she was asking him to be the patron for her, and especially for Naomi. In accepting the proposal, he agreed to provide for them. A woman alone in that culture was vulnerable to violence and abuse, but a woman who had a patron to protect her was safe.

Boaz was probably about Naomi's age. Boaz would have married at the proper age—much younger than he is in our story—and the community's respect for him would have been based in part on his marriage and on having children as a young man. We don't know if he had lost his wife or if Ruth became a second wife, but in either case, Boaz stepped up to provide protection and provision for these oppressed women. In doing so, he became part of the lineage of Jesus—a pretty amazing result.

Yahweh is the Hebrew name for *God*.

Hannah

"God chose what is weakest in the world to shame the strong."
—Terry Eagleton

"Now I have the answers for my enemies; I rejoice because [the Lord] rescued me."
—1 Samuel 2:1b

••••••••••

Many cultures—modern and ancient—honor families. One way that women found honor in ancient times was through children, especially sons. Having no children was devastating to barren women. Never bearing children brought deep shame.

A wedge of hopelessness arises when we can't fix the problem. Such inability plunges us into the icy waters of misery. We can't find a solution and see no better outcome in the future.

Despair often follows hopelessness. Sometimes we rage against those who ought to take care of the problem. Doctors. Parents. Employers. But especially God.

We ask why God hasn't waved a finger and made everything the way we want. And we can become bitter toward God, as Naomi did in the last story.

Something important to notice in Naomi's story was that God never told Naomi, "Well, you blamed me, so now you're getting what you deserve." God remained constant in his kindness and love toward his family of believers.

In our next story, a young wife faces great humiliation. Is there a chance that God will remember her as he remembered her ancestors? She makes a daring request, but what will God do?

··········

The reds and purples of the sunset melted into gray shadows as the family neared Shiloh.

"Elkanah, will we arrive before nightfall?" Hannah leaned close to her husband, enjoying his warmth and holding his arm.

Elkanah had led his household on foot for the last leg of their journey, with the servants and donkeys following. The donkeys carried pack or provisions and two servants tended the sheep brought for the festival sacrifice.

"We need to. The children will probably run ahead, anyway." Elkanah glanced over his shoulder at his 10-year-old son, Pasi, who was already quickening his steps. He was ready to break away from their caravan and run to the town.

Pasi looked back at Elkanah, who nodded permission. Pasi sprinted toward Shiloh.

"Oh, Papa, we want to see the booths! And our friends!" Elkanah's daughter touched his elbow. "Please keep going."

"Oh, I will, Gerar. I want the same things." Elkanah looked down as his three younger children hung close to his robe.

Hannah smiled at the children and reached out to Gerar, but the girl pulled away and ran to her mother.

Peninnah was nearby. She always seemed to be nearby, guarding her children like a snarling wolf. Her offspring had learned to avoid Hannah. Peninnah swung the baby away from Hannah's sight.

Hannah pulled her hand into her robe and lifted her chin, holding the horizon steady in her gaze until the tears evaporated.

The structures of Shiloh jutted into the evening sky. Hannah squinted, trying to locate the booths. Many people had arrived before her own family, making their preparations after erecting their booths.

"Papa, what is the Feast of Tabernacles?" Tavi, the five-year-old, clung to her father's hand and pushed her youthful face into his robes to hide from Hannah.

"Our people remember when our fathers traveled in the wilderness," Elkanah said. "Our fathers built booths to rest in, not houses like ours. They had to keep moving their booths when they marched."

"Where were they going?" Tavi lifted her face from Elkanah's robes long enough to ask.

"To the Promised Land." Elkanah said. "Here. We live in Yahweh's promised land. He gave this land to our fathers."

"But why do we come *here*?" Tavi looked toward Shiloh.

"Our fathers placed the temple to Yahweh here. We come to thank Yahweh for our harvest and to remember that he gave us this land. We had a very good harvest again, Tavi. Yahweh cares for us."

"We are nearly there." Elkanah turned his face to Hannah at his side. "Maybe I'll turn the children loose. Although I think Pasi has already arrived at the camp." He laughed again and picked his youngest daughter. "But you, young Tavi, can stay with your papa for now. Maybe when you're older, you can run with the others."

Elkanah's family never missed a year of celebration. "You honor Yahweh," Hannah said. "You are a good man."

He drew her close. "The harvest was excellent, so we want to thank him."

Yes, Yahweh had provided a rich harvest again. But could she celebrate when she had reaped no harvest? Again. Each month brought the painful reminder that she had no child. Again. She wanted to be grateful to Yahweh for how he provided for her family, but had Yahweh forgotten her?

Was Peninnah right? Had she angered Yahweh? Should she have come? Maybe Yahweh didn't even want her to join those he had blessed? Had he turned his face away from her?

There was still enough light, as they drew near to Shiloh, to see booths draped in green vines and leaves. The smell of campfire smoke filled the air. Just like it had been for her ancestors long ago.

After the family erected their booth, and bits of food were handed out, Elkanah settled near the community fire. "Come with me, Hannah." She nestled close to him, enjoying his warmth and the light of the fire.

"Oh, how much barley and wheat we brought into the threshing floor this year," he said. "It was a good year again. You remember the old stories, don't you?"

"Yes," Hannah whispered. "I remember the old stories. How did our fathers cross the wilderness? It was only sand. No water. No food. But Yahweh provided water and manna."

Elkanah stirred the ground with a small twig and then tossed it into the fire. "I think I am most impressed by what Yahweh did in Egypt. Our people were slaves to the cruel Egyptians. Do you remember they killed the baby boys?"

Hannah remembered and wrapped her arms around herself to still the sudden trembling. The Egyptian cruelty might have been harder to withstand than never bearing a son. To give birth to a son—what an honor—and then see the Egyptians take him.

"Are you cold? Get closer to the fire."

"No, I'm not cold." Hannah mourned those baby boys. Killed before they had a chance. Tears bubbled in her eyes.

"Our people cried out to Yahweh for help and he listened." Elkanah turned suddenly. "I should call the children. They need to hear this."

"Of course." Hannah waited until the children settled on Elkanah's far side, away from her. Their choice stirred a familiar ache in her heart. Like biting into bread, expecting rich flavor but finding air inside.

"Tomorrow is our fellowship offering," Elkanah told his children. "We will roast our offering with the others and share the meat. I will bring each of you a portion and we eat together with our people. Together, we celebrate with Yahweh for what he has done for our fathers."

Hannah quietly slipped away into the darkness. Yahweh remembered her ancestors. But had he forgotten her? She looked over her shoulder as Elkanah taught his children. Peninnah's children. Not hers. Her hands trembled as she walked to their booth.

·········

When the time of the fellowship sacrifice arrived, Elkanah held bits of meat for his family. He brought a portion to Peninnah, but carried twice as much to

Hannah. He touched her hand gently as he handed her the meat.

"For your sacrifice," he said.

Peninnah hissed and glared at Hannah. The fiery stare ignited Hannah's tears yet again. Always the angry looks. Always the tears.

Elkanah glanced at Peninnah and held Hannah's hand. "Why are you crying? Why aren't you eating?"

Words pushed through her tight throat. "I have no children. You know this."

"But you have me," he said. "Am I not better than ten sons?" He kissed her forehead, but his touch didn't still the gnawing in her heart. Pain that none could see but which made her quiver at her loss.

In the evening, people brought tambourines and lyres to the gathering around the crackling bonfire. The leaping flames threw shadows beyond the crowd. Soon the women would dance and then men would tell stories. And laughter would rise like the fire's embers.

Hannah wandered away. Too much happiness. She could only hide her heart for so long.

The sanctuary was dim in the night light, but she walked toward it. Yahweh was there. She knew what he had done for her people. His kindness.

Once, the Egyptians had treated her people as worthless lowlives, as slaves, as nothings.

Like Hannah.

Without a child, she too was nothing—of no value in her village.

Her people had begged Yahweh to help them. When the Egyptians slaughtered their sons and oppressed the nation. Broken. The Israelites cried out to the skies. To a God they couldn't see and barely knew. And he had answered.

He remembered the promises he had made to Abraham and Isaac and Jacob. The Israelites couldn't remember much of him, but Yahweh remembered them. They were his chosen people, and he had answered their calls.

Would Yahweh hear her plea? Hot tears rolled down her cheeks again. Would he notice a barren woman? She had given him nothing. Would he consider her cry for mercy?

She tiptoed to the tabernacle, her stomach gripped by the steel claws of hopelessness. Did she dare ask? Would Yahweh care about her?

In this place where Yahweh lived, Hannah whispered. "O Lord of heaven, you know my sorrow. You know my heart. Please hear me. Please give me a son." Thin words. She had no eloquent songs to sing.

She had asked before. But she would ask again. He remembered her ancestors. Would Yahweh remember her?

She drew in a rattly breath. Then she spoke words she hadn't planned to say. "If you give me a son, I will give him back to you. He will be yours for a lifetime."

If Yahweh gave her a son, she would have something precious to give to Yahweh in thanksgiving. Would he allow her to bear a son? That joy of giving birth to a son who would then serve Yahweh could sustain her.

She opened her eyes to see the priest standing beside her. "Are you drunk, woman?" His voice grated like a knife raked over rough wood.

The revelers near the fire were whooping loudly, and sometimes the celebration of wine got out of hand.

"Oh, no, sir," she said, wiping the tear trails from her face. "I am not drunk." Did she dare tell this man about her troubles? She went for the minimum. She'd had enough pain for one evening.

"I was praying to Yahweh," she whispered. "I am not a wicked woman, but I pray from my pain."

The priest sighed, probably out of relief that he didn't need to deal with an inebriated woman, and smiled. "Well, then, go in peace and may Yahweh answer your prayer." He patted her shoulder and walked away.

His words were like fresh water to her dry heart. "Thank you." She rose and returned to the feast. Had Yahweh heard her cry for help? The priest had given his blessing, and she felt the burden lift like a bird in flight.

Yahweh heard the cries of her forefathers. He could hear her, too.

·········

After the Festival ended, Elkanah and his family returned home. Before many months, Hannah found herself pregnant. A glow filled her days and she walked with a light heart.

This child's movements, as the pregnancy advanced, were strong and determined. "I think Yahweh has given us a son," she said to Elkanah.

"Yahweh is kind," Elkanah said. "May it be."

And so it was. She gave birth to a son.

"Yahweh heard my pain. He remembered me."

Time passed too quickly. When the boy was about three years old, Hannah brought him back to Shiloh.

"Are you sure you want to do this?" Elkanah asked.

"I promised Yahweh that I would do this."

Elkanah kissed the top of her head. "This sacrifice honors Yahweh."

That evening, Hannah danced near the fire with others watching her. She didn't mind if the others saw her because she had no more shame. She knew Yahweh remembered her as he did his chosen children.

Instead, she sang sweet words of love. "There is no one like Yahweh," she said. "He protects his faithful ones. There is no power but Yahweh's power."

She twirled in the bobbing light, shaking a tambourine. The others cheered with her. "I was ashamed," she shouted. "I had no children, but Yahweh has blessed me. He heard me and has taken away my burden and set me free."

On the last day of the Festival, Hannah brought her son to the sanctuary and spoke to the high priest.

She had packed a small bag of the boy's favorites, his robes and blankets. She whispered to the high priest. "You may not remember me, but I have kept my promise to Yahweh."

The high priest nodded. He had been told that this event was coming. He grasped Hannah's hands. "We will care for your son. And I believe he will grow to be a man of strength. A man to serve Yahweh."

The boy's eyes brimmed with love for his parents, but they had also prepared him for this moment. He stood straight and stepped closer to the high priest.

The high priest patted him on the head. "What is the boy's name?"

"His name is Samuel," Hannah said.

"Ah, yes," the high priest smiled. He gathered the boy to his side and met Hannah's gaze. "You remembered what Yahweh did in the past. The boy's name means 'Yahweh has heard.' And so he does. And so he has."

············

Digging Deeper:

Have you felt deep hopelessness, like Hannah's sorrow? If so, describe some emotions you felt during that time.

In hard times, have you known a Peninnah, who inflicted more pain? Or maybe you've been a Peninnah. How does this story help in dealing with someone who intensifies hopelessness?

If you're not familiar with the story of the Israelites while in slavery in Egypt, you can read about their plea for help in Exodus 2:22-25. Yahweh responded to their cries for help. How did he respond to Hannah's cry for help?

You can read Hannah's story in 1 Samuel 1. Based on Hannah's story, how would you define hope?

Behind the Scenes
Samuel grew up to be the last judge and a godly leader among the Israelites. God blessed Hannah with three more sons and two daughters. (1 Samuel 2:21). Penninah was probably a second wife taken in when Hannah could not bear children, a common occurrence in ancient times.

At the time of Elkanah and Hannah, the Ark of the Covenant was at the sanctuary in Shiloh. The high priest, Eli, and his sons, Hophni and Phinehas, were dishonest and Yahweh dealt strongly with them.

Several of the judges sent by God to lead his people descended into inadequacy or even idolatry. But God, through Samuel, renewed Israel at Shiloh—the very place where these priests were corrupting the worship at the sanctuary.

The sacrifices of this story were fellowship sacrifices. The Israelites offered all of a burnt offering to Yahweh but, with a fellowship offering, some of the offering went to Yahweh and the people shared the rest. This was like a barbecue in which Yahweh and his family split the meat. Elkanah, as head of his family, would then divide his fellowship offering with all members of his family. He gave a double share to Hannah to show his love for her.

Daniel's Journey

"Shame should be reserved for the things we choose to do, not the circumstances that life puts on us."
—Ann Patchett

"Blessed be the name of God from age to age, for wisdom and power are his."
—Daniel 2:20

In the previous story, Hannah learned God had not forgotten her despite her barrenness.

Hannah hung onto hope because she believed that, if God had heard and rescued her ancestors, he could do the same thing for her. And when he did, she responded with the same joy and celebration she had learned from her ancestors.

Hannah found hope by looking into the past: what God had done before, he would do again.

In our next story, hopeless seems the only logical response. Other gods and empires appear to have defeated God. Is he as strong as his people think? Is there hope for the people of God if God seems weak?

·········

Smoldering smoke from the dying city smudged the blue sky behind Daniel as he and his friends trudged forward on the wide trail. Spears pierced the sky above their heads.

"How could this happen?" Hevel walked beside Daniel and leaned toward him. "We are Yahweh's people. Did he forget us?"

"He didn't forget us." Daniel licked dusty lips with a dry tongue. The drumbeat of heavy sandals thickened the air.

"If that's true," Hevel said, "then he wasn't strong enough."

Daniel could see a wagon ahead lurching from side to side, filled with prizes from the temple. The Babylonians left ash and rubble behind them but brought the rich treasures.

"The temple is gone. They leveled it. And they stole all the worship items. They're going to melt down the gold and silver. Why couldn't Yahweh defend his house?"

"At least we're alive," Daniel said.

"Who knows what they are going to do to us?" Hevel spit on the ground and a Babylonian soldier shoved him forward a few steps. He slowed a little, his feet shuffling through the dusty road.

"I wonder if we'll ever go home." Daniel whispered. "Did you hear about King Zedekiah?"

Hevel snorted. "Yahweh didn't protect him either. I heard the Babylonians carried him to Babylon after they poked out his eyes. He went in chains. Where was Yahweh when this happened?"

"He hasn't forgotten us." Daniel wanted to sound brave, but the words were hollow even to him.

"Where do you think we're going?" Havel said. "Babylon?"

"Probably."

A soldier growled and poked the butt end of his spear into Daniel's back. "Keep walking." Daniel lowered his head and did not glance back.

"I want to ask that soldier who their gods are," Havel said. "It looks like their gods are stronger than Yahweh."

"How can you say this? Yahweh has condemned other idols."

"Yeah, well, I'm not so sure that Yahweh is stronger when these other gods strike. Notice what what happened when the Babylonians came to Jerusalem. Their gods helped them destroy our city and Yahweh's temple. They won."

Daniel's legs were dead meat, and his mouth was dry like drinking sand. Would they get any more water today? "Remember our feasts in the palace?"

Havel snorted. "Really? You want to talk about food? We were royals then. We're prisoners now."

Distractions can help, and Daniel ran hard after one. "Remember the grapes? The roasted lamb? The cakes?"

"We'll see nothing like that again," Havel said. "We're probably going to be tortured in a dungeon somewhere. A Babylonian dungeon. I wonder how ugly those are."

"I don't want to talk about that."

Havel snickered. "Just pleasant thoughts, eh? You need to face facts. Our lives are over. The only hope I can see is to join the Babylonians in their worship."

"What? Have you forgotten who we are?"

"Have you noticed how they honor their gods? They carry them along the way and stop for times of prayer. They've very devoted. I can see why." Havel shook his head and dust billowed from his dusty hair into Daniel's face. Daniel sneezed. "Their gods won."

In front of them, the long line of prisoners snaked down the road. Some soldiers rode along the column, but most of the soldiers marched with long sharp spears and scanned the clusters of captives close to them.

The Babylonian priests were at the front of the line. The honored position.

"Don't you remember what our prophets told us?" Daniel said. "We shouldn't worship idols. That's probably why Yahweh let us be conquered."

"Or he isn't strong enough for these gods. These are very impressive idols."

∙∙∙∙∙●∙●∙∙∙

The group marched day-by-soul-crushing day until a morning came when the prisoners cleared a small ridge to see a vast city sprawled before them. Tall spires and towering structures filled the valley below and green trees framed lofty gates. Lush trees in the desert? How had these people accomplished this?

"Whoa! What is this city? Breath-taking!" Havel said.

"I suppose it is Babylon. I didn't expect this."

"You expected something like Jerusalem, didn't you?" Havel stumbled because he tried to stop and was pushed forward by a guard. He shrugged his shoulders and stared as he walked. "This is the city of a powerful empire. And a strong king. Do you see all the wealth of this place? Not like what we had in Jerusalem."

The walls of the city soared into the sky. Massive brick walls loomed and enormous gates punctuated the powerful exterior of the facade. Green leaves gripped columns. Fruit trees dotted the horizon.

"Gardens!" Havel said. "In the desert. Gardens and water. If we live, I want to stay here."

Daniel could see another structure with its spire spiking the clouds. "What is that?" He dared not point with a soldier at his shoulder.

"I think that's a temple," Havel said. "Wow, what an impressive building."

"Solomon built a beautiful temple, too."

"Which is now a smoldering pile of rubble." Havel elbowed Daniel lightly. "We got trounced, my friend."

They made their way through the wide and towering gate. Soldiers poked at them, directing them to another majestic building of stone and wood and painted murals. There they waited in a massive courtyard.

Men in flowing orange or blue robes passed through the group of dirty exiles, studying faces and touching ribs.

"You're a royal. Go with him." A man tapped Daniel on the shoulder and pointed to a long stone passageway. There, a small group of Jews was gathering. Picked by the Robe Men, apparently. Daniel stepped toward the group.

The coolness of the stone floors gave new life to Daniel's tired feet. Servants robed in fresh robes brought trays of cold water in carved clay cups. Others offered plates of figs, pomegranates, apples, and melons.

He touched his face to feel the filth caked on his cheeks and chin. The ash of Jerusalem and the temple still clung to his cheeks.

Refresh the inside first. He ate and drank his fill.

Then a young man grasped his elbow. "Come this way. We have a room for you and I have drawn your bath. There are new clothes as well." He kept talking as he walked. "I am Buzur, your servant."

"How has this happened?" Daniel studied this young Babylonian servant, wearing a clean short robe and promising him a room and a bath. Daniel was a prisoner of war and yet this was provided for him?

"The king, may he live forever, supplies these for you." Buzur lead the way to a large room with long orange drapery over windows and a soft bed piled high with thick pillows. Several polished wooden cabinets lined the walls, topped by painted vases. A basin of steaming water drew Daniel's eye. A bath too?

Buzur helped Daniel discard the old clothes. Buzur threw them in a heap near the door, and a second servant silently carried them away. Daniel never saw his Jerusalem garb again. No matter now. The bath drew his attention. He stepped into the tub, letting the steam wrap his body in moist warmth. The faint smell of pine needles drifted from the water, and he closed his eyes as he lay back into the water.

"Allow me," Buzur began scrubbing Daniel's skin, releasing the dirt and ash and sweat with fragrant soaps and soft towels. After the scrubbing, which involved much effort, Buzur then dressed Daniel in new robes. Babylonian silk. Cool and smooth. Silk in Jerusalem was very rare.

"Tomorrow," Buzur said, "you will begin your training. The king has chosen the best from your people to become advisors to him. You are one of the chosen ones."

Daniel stared. "I am still young. I haven't completed my education yet."

"You'll be trained here, educated by our best scholars who will teach you about the king's administration. You were training for that in your homeland since you're of royal blood. Weren't you?"

On the trail, hopelessness had pressed down like the stinking smoke of Jerusalem's fires. Hope for a future seemed impossible. But now, maybe, there was a future. Daniel slept deeply in his new bed.

In the morning, Daniel arose and waited for Buzur to return.

"I have exciting news." Buzur rushed into the room and clapped his hands together. Apparently applauding the news. Was this a Babylonian custom? "The king will meet your class this morning. He has important announcements."

Daniel ate a breakfast of juicy fruit and then joined the other students in the great hall. Heavy purple and gold tapestry hung on the walls. Torches illuminated the room and uniformed soldiers stood along the walls.

Daniel studied the other students to see if he knew anyone. He spotted Mishael. They had been friends in Jerusalem, but the crowd separated them at the moment. Some Jews and mostly Babylonian young men milled around. Before Daniel could try to press through the crowd, a short trumpet blast interrupted the young men.

Others looked toward the front of the room, and so Daniel turned, too.

The king stood on a platform above them, his robes glittering with silver trim and expensive embroidery. Green vines and yellow flowers burst from great vases beside him. "Some of you know me already and some will learn today about me. I am your king," he said, and walked from side to side on the platform. His servants followed with large feathered fans and plates of fruit and meat, careful to stay out of his way when he turned back. Was he showing off his power over the servants?

"I am the greatest king this world has ever seen. Do you doubt it? You Jews. Do you remember your city? Poof, I conquered it like this." The king waved his hand from side to side as one would extinguish a candle. He studied the room, his head turning from side to side. Then he continued talking, his deep voice echoing in the big room. His voice filled every corner and crevice.

"I'm your future now. I will train you and you will serve me. You will live in the palace and share my own servants. *My* food. *My* accommodations."

Daniel watched the king continue pacing on the platform, his robes flowing freely behind him, as he formed his next points of the speech. Servants formed an obedient line behind him, turning when he turned, anticipating every twitch. He thrust out his hand and a place of figs immediately appeared. He didn't glance down as he selected the fruit and tossed it in his mouth.

The king's voice boomed into the crowd, driving his words through the young men standing before him. Daniel peeked to each side. The other students appeared hypnotized by the king's speech.

"I am the son of the gods. We honor our gods highly. You will learn of our gods in the classes. Consider yourselves honored to be here, trained in my palace, for service to me."

He clapped his hands together, and a bevy of servants leaned forward in readiness, like greyhounds primed for the rabbit's release. "Tonight, we will have a feast featuring the best foods from my kitchen. You have had a long journey and I will restore your strength. You will feast on my delicious delicacies."

Daniel drew a deep breath. So this was to be his life, as a counsellor to the king. Sumptuous food. Rich clothing. Extravagant education. This, surely, was hope restored. He wouldn't be killed or tortured or forced into hard labor. He would use his mind and his education in service to the king.

This was not so different from the path he had been on with his training at home. Because of his royal blood, the advisors had expected him to serve the king in Jerusalem.

When the show ended, Daniel returned to his room.

"Buzur, my feasts at home featured venison and turkey, ham and roast beef. All sorts of fruits and pies. Cakes. Puddings. Will it be so here?"

Buzur clapped his hands together. "Much more. Everything is better here. You will grow strong with the king's food. The king will make you strong and ready to learn."

And then, unexpectedly, Mishael stepped into the room.

"You are here." Daniel rushed to his friend and clasped his forearms. "I thought they had killed you in Jerusalem."

"I thought the same about you, too." Mishael smiled. He had been washed and fed and apparently allowed to visit.

"We are safe. That's something."

"Many of us are safe. The king has plans to use us." Mishael picked up a carved vase. "Beautiful art work.

The architecture here is beyond our knowledge. So I wonder why they want us."

"It's easy to control our people if they see familiar faces like us representing the king," Daniel said. "How do you feel about the king's food?"

Mishael snorted. "It's unclean."

"I doubt that will be a consideration," Daniel said. "I have another concern with it."

"Which is?"

"The king told us he will make us strong. His food will give us our health back. That's what he says, and that's what he will tell our people when we are seen healthy and strong."

Mishael sank into a heap of soft pillows. "These beds are better than sleeping on the ground. I like that. But I understand your concern about the food. The king will get the credit. It's another way to control our people."

"I have a plan," Daniel said.

"To escape?"

"No. We'll never escape. But I don't believe that Yahweh has forgotten us. I propose a test to show which king is greater."

"Which king?"

"Nebuchadnezzar, king of Babylon, or Yahweh, king of the world."

Mishael reached for an ornate jug and poured water into a cup. "When you put it that way... What is your plan?"

"We eat our own food. Not the king's food."

"Which will prove...."

"What if, in two weeks, we appear better than the other men? Won't that prove which king is stronger?"

Buzur had been standing motionless in the corner, but now he stepped forward. "I could die if you do this. If you are more haggard than the others, the king will blame me."

"But what if it works? What if Yahweh is truly powerful?" Daniel turned to his servant.

Buzur twisted his mouth from side to side. "What would you eat?"

"Vegetables and water. None of the king's rich foods. If you see that we're declining on Yahweh's food, you can end the experiment."

"We can try it." Buzur nodded. "But I will end this quickly if I see one rib grow more prominent. I'm not taking a risk on a new god."

The days rolled by in a regular regimen of lectures, reading, and writing. Daniel and the other students met in a large room with tables, chairs and stern instructors who lectured for long hours and then gave difficult tests.

The king did not come to the group again. Was he out with his army, conquering new nations? Buzur confirmed this. The king was not in the palace, and so Buzur was safe for the moment.

Then the day came when Buzur faced Daniel and looked him up and down. "You have more muscle. And the color of your face is healthy. I saw you wrestle well during training yesterday." He exhaled. "Your God is making you strong."

Daniel slapped his back. "I'm glad you can see the difference. I feel it, too."

When the king returned from his military battles, he gathered the young men to test them. They all stood again in the great room as the king paraded in front of them. He surveyed the group of students. "You." He pointed at Daniel. "You're the best. And your friends as well. I knew this training regimen was a great idea. I always know. You'll join my magicians and advisors. Someday you may even surpass them. I knew this system of mine would work. I always know."

But the king didn't know what Buzur and the other servants knew. The king didn't know what the young trainees knew. He had not yet seen what Yahweh would do.

No false gods had defeated Yahweh, and he had not abandoned his people even in the depths of hardship. Daniel lost his family and his homeland, but God never forgot him.

••••••••••

Digging Deeper

Read the story of Daniel's first challenge in Babylon in Daniel 1.

Some Israelites wondered if a stronger force had beaten Yahweh. Can you think of a time when God seemed to be defeated? How did that affect your faith in God?

Daniel trusted Yahweh even when outside forces seemed to defeat him. When things looked impossible, some (like Havel) decided that the way forward was to follow a new god and a new king. Daniel remained true to God. How does Daniel's story help you understand hope in seemingly impossible circumstances?

We sometimes assume that we are safe if the right government is in power or the right economic system is dominant. Daniel chose not to trust in an empire, no matter how powerful, but to trust in God. How does that encourage you in your day-to-day choices?

Behind the Scenes
The story of Daniel refusing the king's food may be familiar to you, but the reason that Daniel chose vegetables and water is unclear. Often we're told it was because he insisted on kosher foods, but if

so, why refrain from wine? Jews did not consider it unclean.

Some have suggested that perhaps the food was first offered to gods before serving it to the king's people. If so, why were vegetables acceptable?

Did Daniel refuse the food as a political statement, a form of passive rebellion? If so, the king apparently never heard of it. Only Daniel and his friends, plus the attendant, knew of the victory.

I have suggested in this story that Daniel saw this offer of the king's food as a ploy to lure them away from God. Daniel, instead, illustrated for himself and the others in his small group that God could do more than the king of the massive Babylonian empire.

The primary message—that God was greater than the king—is clear even when we're unsure about Daniel's motivation.

Grasping At Crumbs

"How far would you go to keep the hope of love alive?"
—Nicholas Sparks

"Now go home, for the demon has left your daughter."
—Jesus in Mark 7:29

· · · · • • • · · ·

The future was dissolving into the smoke of staggering defeat for Daniel in the last chapter. He experienced what looked like a sheer thrashing of his nation and of his God.

But Daniel did not abandon God, and he didn't abandon his future. He discovered God had not forsaken him, but protected him from the early days of his life to the end. Because of his faithfulness, Daniel witnessed God doing impossible things.

Hope is about the future, and what we trust it will be. Having confidence in the future may seem easy when things are going our way.

But sometimes the future looks unimaginable. We join a mother who can't fix her beloved daughter's problem. She looks for help in a new place - and seems to be turned away. Does hope remain?

This mother persists when all seems lost. Grasping for hope for a loved one changes her. Can hope win out?

· · · · • • • · · ·

The shriek split the morning cool and interrupted Udiya's bread making. She turned from her table, blinking at the yellow morning sun pouring through the doorway of the mud hut.

Reva. Her daughter dashed through the doorway and seemed to assault the room with pounding feet, her hair tangled like a lion's mane. She reached out with talons for fingers. "Food. Give me food." Her howls sliced through the morning's quiet.

"Reva! You're naked! Let me get a covering for you." Udiya hurried to the corner to pick up a thin blanket. "What are you doing?" Udiya had not seen her daughter in several weeks.

"I am hungry. Give me food. Now. Food." Reva continued to shriek, her head turning rapidly from side to side. Then she saw the dough that Udiya had dropped on the table. Udiya tried to spread the blanket over her naked daughter, but Reva shoved her with both hands. "Get away!" And then Reva ran out of the hut.

Udiya followed for a few steps. "I have food for you." But it was too late. Reva was gone.

Once she had tried to grab her daughter, but Riva had slammed her mother to the ground. The bruises had only just faded from that meeting.

Udiya only knew Reva lived somewhere on the rocky hill outside their village, but Udiya would not follow today.

It had been this way for too long. What was she eating? The food must be scarce if she would risk barging into her parents' house.

"Was that Reva?" a girl whispered, and Udiya turned to her younger daughter. Emet tiptoed around the corner of the house, her dark hair covered with a brown scarf.

"I'm sorry you had to see that. Yes, it was Reva." Udiya felt hot tears form, but there was work to be done. She wiped her face with her hand and marched back to her house. She picked up the dough, gripping it between clenched fists.

"I miss her," Emet said. "Did she find food?"

"No, she ran away before I could give her anything."

Emet settled to the floor and threw an arm around Dodi, their brown dog. She gently stroked Dodi's soft fur. "She ran away with the blanket."

"She did?" Udiya hadn't noticed.

"What's wrong with her?" Emet, at 13, didn't understand her sister.

"I think she has a demon." Udiya kneaded the dough with both hands. Squeezing the dough harder than it needed. Slamming it down on the table. Pounding it with the side of her fist. "An evil spirit. It owns her heart and mind."

"You need a god to throw out an evil spirit."

Udiya looked at the shelf where their household idols stood. "Some gods they are. I don't think they help any. They haven't yet." She began flattening the dough with the heels of her hands. She should send Emet to get some wood for the cooking fire, but she wanted to talk to someone.

"Why can't our gods work for Reva?"

"Here's what I've noticed. The craftsman brings a log to his shop. He cuts it in two parts. He chisels half of it into an idol. Then he takes the rest of the log and burns it to keep him warm. That makes no sense to me."

Emet looked up at the ceiling for a minute. Thinking. "Are all the gods made of wood like that?"

"Not all. But most of our people are too poor for the ones made of silver. Those are for the rich."

"Would a rich man's idol work better?"

Udiya laughed suddenly. "We'd certainly never be able to get one, even if that was true. We are too poor." There were a few twigs close to the fire, and she tossed them in. Were those bits of wood mini idols? The thought made her laugh again. "There's more. I've seen idols that can't stand. They collapse and then the craftsman has to nail them to chunk of wood or they'd fall over."

GRASPING AT CRUMBS 51

Emet laughed. "Silly gods." And then she covered her mouth. "What if they can hear us?"

"If they can't stand alone, I don't know why they'd be able to hear us." Udiya rubbed the small of her back, feeling stiffness after leaning over the table.

"So, what can we do for Reva?" Emet fluffed Dodi's fur. "I miss her. This is so sad for her. Isn't there a god who can kick out that evil spirit?"

"There's a man." Udiya scanned the room for her next chore. "I talked with some travelers and they told me about this man in the south who has healed blind people. He made a paralyzed man walk. He cured sick people. They claimed he had cast out demons, too."

"Let's take Reva to him." Emet laid her face on Dodi's neck. "I think Dodi misses her, too."

Then Emet got to her feet and pinched off a piece of dough for Dodi to eat. At Udiya's stern look, she shrugged. "He's hungry, too. We can share a little food with him."

Udiya shrugged. Yes, they could share.

"This teacher has made me curious. I don't think he's a traveling magician." Udiya remembered a magician who had visited the town a few weeks before. He'd come with bright robes and fancy talk. Asking a fee before he did any of his work. Tricks for money.

"What does this teacher charge for his magic?"

"Nothing."

Emet picked up a small broom, but clearly she didn't want to continue her morning chores. "I don't think Reva would go to him," she said. "She's not going anywhere. She won't even come home."

"Let's go gather some wood." Gathering tinder was usually Emet's job, but Udiya didn't want to be alone this morning. They stepped out of the hut and made their way to the edge of town, searching for bits of wood.

"What if the teacher came here? Maybe we could trick Reva into coming to him?" Emet was still plotting.

"I wonder why he would come here," Udiya said. "He's a Jew. They hate us."

"I heard a story once about the Jews' God and our people," Emet said. "I don't think their God hates us."

"I've heard stories, too. I heard about a woman a long time ago. When the Jews first came to Canaan. They were ready to invade Jericho, and she believed they would destroy her city."

"Why did she believe that?"

"She heard stories about the Jewish God. That's what I was told. Stories about their God and the miraculous things he'd done. He even fed them in the desert. So, I guess she believed them."

"A Gentile believed in the Jewish god." Emet didn't ask another question. "Stories help, don't they?"

Udiya bent to the parched soil to pick up a small branch. "What would we do without stories? That woman was saved because she believed the stories. She wasn't a Jew, but she believed. The Jewish God protected her."

There were few trees here, and they'd soon be burning other things beside wood. But today, there was still a little wood and Emet's arms filled with what they found.

"Do you think the teacher is a god?" Emet said. "It sounds like he's doing things a god would do."

A man as a god? Udiya stood and faced Emet. "He is doing impossible things, isn't he? Our gods can't do what he is doing. I hear the Jews talk about a messiah, a man who would come."

Emet's face lit up, and she clapped her hands together. "That's who he is, isn't it? The Jewish Messiah."

Udiya grabbed Emet's elbows to hold her close. She stared into Emet's chocolate eyes. "We don't know that. He might just be another magician." Then she smiled and released Emet. Ran her hand along her daughter's cheek. "But we'd like that if he was, wouldn't we?"

"I think he is." Emet met Udiya's gaze and returned her smile.

Udiya put her arm around her daughter's shoulder. "But there was another story. From the travelers. A wild story. They claim that the teacher had a large crowd listening to him teach. There wasn't food for the crowd. Just a little boy's lunch. But the teacher prayed over the food and broke it into pieces to give to the crowd. And there was enough for everyone. Plus leftovers."

"Those were pretty tiny pieces." Emet laughed and Udiya laughed with her. They began walking back to the town then. The midday air heated in the midday sun.

"I like that story," Emet said. "It's like the story about God feeding his people in the wilderness. Who is this teacher who does what God does?"

"You think deep thoughts, my daughter."

"Let's believe he is God," Emet said. "For Reva's sake. I want to believe in this Jewish God. What have we to lose?"

"If this teacher is God, then he is the Son of God and the son of King David," Udiya said. "He is everything the Jews have been waiting for. I wonder if there's hope for us, too."

"Like the woman at Jericho?" Emet winked at her mother and leaned into her for a moment.

Then it was time to work on meal preparations before her husband and sons came in from the fields to eat. They worked hard and came home hungry.

She'd need more than bread for them. There was work yet to do and no more time for talking.

Reva didn't return to the house that day. Or any days to come.

"May I leave bits of food at the edge of town?" Emet asked. "In case Reva appears there? I've watched for her, but she doesn't come."

Udiya nodded. "Even a small amount might keep her alive."

··········

Days turned into weeks into months, with no end in sight. No future for Reva. No hope.

Then one day, there was a commotion in town. Udiya could hear voices calling out. She stepped outside and saw her neighbor standing across the way. "What is happening?"

"That Jewish teacher is in town," the neighbor said. "Who knows why he is here? Did he get lost? There are no Jews here."

Udiya ran on the hard-packed streets until she saw the crowd. She lifted her long robe to give her feet room for the race. Hope had been a cold ember but there was a faint warmth in her heart. Could she convince Reva to meet the teacher? Would he wait while she tried?

Udiya entered the town plaza, searching the small stone houses around the edge.

She spotted Jewish men standing outside a house. He must be there. There were no other Jews were in town.

Did this teacher know someone in the village?

It didn't matter to her why he had come to her town. She kept running, her sandals drumming on the hard ground. No one looked her way.

How would she get past the men? They wouldn't let her into the house. A Gentile woman? No chance. But she couldn't give up. Maybe she could catch the teacher's attention. Show her belief.

"Have mercy on me, my Lord. You are the Son of David. Have mercy!" She shouted. This might be Reva's only chance.

Udiya was nearly at the house now, shouting the phrases over and over.

She hadn't asked for anything except mercy, but she wanted more. Could this teacher release her daughter? Could she find a way to ask?

She barrelled through the doorway, past the men standing idly at the side, into the center of the room.

Although the room was dark with only slits to let in a little light, she could see a man seated at a table with a plate before him. Roasted grains and fruits.

Now was the time. She shouted again. "A demon torments my daughter. It's horrible, my Lord."

He ignored her.

His men closed around him to protect him from this unclean Gentile woman. "Send her away," they said. "She is just a beggar."

Udiya could not lose this chance to help her daughter. She pressed forward, ready to fight with the disciples if they thought they'd stop her. For Reva.

Then the teacher turned to her. "I was only sent for God's lost sheep—for Israel." His voice was gentle, and he studied her face.

She fell to the ground. Even if he wouldn't help her, she could worship him. She needed to believe that he was the true God and she wanted to follow the truth. "Please help me." This may be Reva's only chance.

"Do you think I should take food away from the children and give it to dogs?" The teacher dabbed his lips with a cloth and cocked his head to one side. Still studying her face.

Well, that was an interesting point. Was his power limited to the Jews? Did he not have enough power to help with both Jews and Gentiles?

She remembered the story about how the teacher had fed a crowd of five thousand with only five loaves of bread and two fish. With leftovers. There had been more than enough.

Just then, little Dodi darted into the house. He'd followed her, silly dog. He licked her ankle and flopped onto the ground. She ignored him. "I agree, my Lord. You came for the Jews."

She remembered how Dodi would lick up any food that was dropped beneath the family table at mealtime. He usually settled in around the toddlers because they dropped more food. He scooped up the extra.

The teacher was still watching her. Udiya's words burst through the air. "But the dogs may eat the scraps that fall from their masters' table."

The teacher glanced down at Dodi, and a gentle smile lifted the corners of his mouth. "Dear woman, you understand much." He studied Udiya's eyes. Then he spoke clearly. "Your faith is great. Your daughter is healed."

That was it? Udiya expected Jesus to call for her daughter and put his hands on her. Maybe speak a special incantation. Maybe pour some oil over her.

Or at least bless her like he had the loaves and fishes.

He hadn't asked for money though.

She got to her feet, ignoring the eyes of the disciples. Did they approve of their teacher's words? Had his words done something miraculous?

She had to find Reva.

Udiya sprinted to her hut and grabbed Emet. "Come. We need to see what the teacher has done."

Together, they raced toward the hills, lifting skirts enough to free their feet. There were no aching muscles in Udiya's legs this day.

Udiya's breath came hard by the time she saw a person running toward her through the shimmering waves of heat.

"Oh." Udiya stopped running. Fear gripped her throat. Who was this? What new danger appeared?

"Mother?" Emet grabbed her elbow. "It's Reva. We can't stop."

Of course, it was Reva. But fear gripped Udiya's heart. "She's hurt me before."

"Not this time." Emet reached out to her mother, pulling her forward again.

They met near an acacia tree, with a stretch of tall brown grass running back to the hills. Reva had slung the blanket over her shoulders. She trembled even though the heat baked them and tried to pull the blanket over her body. Tears washed rivulets in her dirty face and words came in bursts. "Mother. Help me."

Udiya reached out. Put her arms around her daughter and pulled her close, feeling Reva's heart pound against her chest. "Tell me what has happened."

"It was like waking up from a nightmare." Reva leaned her forehead into Udiya's shoulder. "I was sitting on a rock. Filthy. And..." She looked down at herself. "I am so ashamed, Mother. I had no clothing. There are bruises everywhere. They hurt. I was in a cave of darkness with something screaming at me. Calling me horrible names. Echoing inside my head."

"But the voices are gone?" Udiya had to be sure.

"Yes, gone."

"How could he could cast out a demon from so far away?" Udiya stroked her daughter's mess of dark hair.

"What is distance when you have plenty?" Emet said, rubbing Reva's back. "He has plenty for all of us."

"Enough for Gentiles? Even dogs?" Udiya said. The teacher's words still rang in her mind.

"I suppose even for Dodi." Emet scowled. Puzzled. But she had not heard the teacher's remarks. "But enough especially for Reva."

••••••••••

Digging In

Have you experienced heartbreak like Udiya? Or known someone who has? How did that impact your thoughts about the future?

Jesus appeared to refuse Udiya, but she pressed on, trusting the stories she had heard about him. What do you do when God seems to refuse to do what you ask for?

Have you ever thought God didn't have enough of something (power/resources/love) for you? What did that do to your hope? How does this story help you know God always has enough?

Behind the scenes

The story of the Syro-Phoenician woman is found in Matthew 15:21-28 and in Mark 7:24-30. I based much of the description of Reva on the story of the demon-possessed man at Gerasenes, found in Luke 8:26-39.

Although we're often taught that the term "dog" in the gospel accounts is an insult to the Gentiles, the Greek word for dog is *kynarion*, which means *little dog*. Gentiles often had dogs as pets, although the Jews didn't. This story takes place in Gentile land and the family pet snatching up dropped food probably happened. And it makes sense to us today as well.

Udiya's comments about idols reflect Old Testament sentiment regarding idols. For example, Isaiah 40:18-26 and Isaiah 41:6-7 ridicule the pagan idols.

The Earthquake

"Courage is like love; it must have hope for nourishment."
Napoleon Bonaparte
"Believe in the Lord Jesus and you will be saved."
Paul in Acts 16:31

············

Udiya faced apparent hopelessness at every turn. A demon ensnared her daughter. And then the teacher seemed to reject her plea for help. Those are times when it's easy to give up.

Udiya's love for her daughter—and her newfound belief in God—gave her hope.

Hardships happen with various intensity, but difficulties don't have to steal away our hope and our future. In this story, we meet a retired Roman soldier with a well-planned future until something unexpected ripped all hope away. How will he continue when he can see no future?

・・・●●・●・・・

Stephanas drained the last of his steaming stew and wiped his mouth with the back of his hand. The thick soup warmed his belly, but the best part of the meal was sharing it with his son.

"Did you eat?" Stephanas turned his gaze. Drusus was thin like many six-year-olds, but he waited until Stephanas invited him to eat.

"No, Father." The boy's eyes brightened when Stephanas handed him a bowl.

They sat at the edge of the street in the cool evening air. The pungent smells of the meat shops were fading and most of the small stone shops were closed for the day. A few people walked silently along the narrow road. A little gray donkey stood tethered to the pillar in front of the incense shop.

"Your mother cooks better than the army cooks."

"I wish I had been alive then. I could have gone with you."

Stephanas laughed. "The stories aren't enough for you?"

Drusus shrugged, digging into the stew.

Stephanas drank deeply from his cup. "I'm glad to be done, though. I get to be here with you." He looked through the door into the cramped jail room with thick stone walls and narrow windows. He spoke more to himself. "The Romans did me right."

THE EARTHQUAKE   63

Then Stephanas looked above Drusus' head, along the street where he could see a group of Roman guards dragging two men. Soldiers had hooked their hands under the arms of the prisoners. Towing them along so the prisoners' toes dug furrows in the lane's dust.

More business. Stephanas rubbed his hands together.

"Drusus, take the food and go inside the house. I have work to do."

Drusus glanced over his shoulder. "Could I stay?"

Stephanas could see the dried blood caked on the two prisoners' faces. Blood from wounds had trickled in dark rivulets.

Better for business. The guards would probably toss these two in his dungeon, and he charged more for the dungeon than the cells on the main level.

"This can get ugly. Go." He waited until Drusus gathered the eating vessels and scurried into the door of their house before he stood to meet the soldiers. "More prisoners?"

"These men started a riot." The first guard's voice was guttural. Grunting. Like a pig. "You should have seen the marketplace. A big riot."

"These two started all that?" Stephanas studied the two prisoners. They looked subdued. Weak. Not capable of starting a riot.

"They were teaching illegal customs." Pig Guard shook a limp prisoner. "Good thing the mayor showed up. He got things under control again."

"These are Jews. What are they doing in Philippi?"

"Causing trouble. What else do Jews do?" Pig Guard elbowed his limp prisoner again.

"They've obviously been beaten. Mayor's orders?"

"Oh, yeah. I think their outer robes are somewhere in the mob. We stripped them and used wooden rods. I'll bet they will think twice before starting trouble like that again." The guard slapped the back of a prisoner's head, just because he could. The prisoners had not even raised their heads.

"And now they are in jail?" Stephanas pulled out his logbook and quill. This would add to his daily charges to the city officials. A good day for business.

"The mayor wants them held overnight. Make sure they don't escape." Pig Guard lifted his chin as though to lord it over on Stephanas. Only he was shorter, so the intimidation ploy didn't work well. He raised his eyes to meet Stephanas' eyes. "Keep them in prison."

"Don't I always?" Stephanas was already sizing up the two prisoners. The chains showed what the mayor thought of them. If they had any status, they wouldn't be in chains. But what Jews had status, anyway?

Lowlifes, then. Men who deserved nothing.

Stephanas had a few other prisoners in the dungeon. A couple more crowded the cell. Good. More misery.

He called his servants.

"Put them in the stocks,' he said. "Keep the chains on. They need to be here in the morning."

THE EARTHQUAKE 65

The servant gave the men a shove, and one fell to his knees. He struggled to get up, and the servant yanked him to his feet. Shoved him again.

Stephanas hoped these Jews survived the night. There would be trouble if they didn't.

"Stocks for these two?" The servant raised an eyebrow. "They can't run."

"The stocks are insurance. We need to be sure." Plus, Stephanas could charge the city officials extra for using the stocks.

Stephanas himself avoided descending into the dungeon when he could. It was dark even at the noon and the stench of body odors offended his senses. Clammy air that never saw the sun.

The floors were jagged and rough. And the stink slithered through the dungeon doors. He sent his servants into that pit. If there was an underworld, it was like the dungeon. He wasn't going unless there was a need. And there wasn't a need.

The servants dragged the two limp men down a few stone stairs and disappeared from sight for a time. Muffled voices and thumps rose from the dungeon. When they returned, they marched up to Stephanas.

"Can they move in the stocks?" Stephanas asked.

"No, sir. They'll be so stiff by morning that they'll only crawl out. If they can move at all. Assuming the mayor even calls for them."

"Oh, he'll call. He'll probably have them executed." Stephanas surveyed the dingy little jail. Good enough for prisoners. "The other prisoners are secure, yes? I'm going to sleep for a while. I'll relieve you later in the night."

Stephanas' jail adjoined his house and his bed was only a few steps from the door to the dungeon.

But he went into a different world as he entered his home. The jail was dark. Thick with odors. But when he closed to the door to his home, he breathed in scented air. Tapestries. Polished wood furniture. All thanks to his wife's touch.

This was the world he wanted.

Stephanas had not slept long when sounds shook him awake. Music? No, singing. He had experienced a lot of things on the battlefields, but nothing like this. Groans frequently drifted from the prison, but never singing. He stood to get closer.

Drusus was at his side.

"You're awake?" Stephanas wrapped his arm around his son's shoulders.

"Why are they singing? Are these the new prisoners?"

"They ought to be unconscious." Stephanas wished he could take back his words, which were harsh for six-year-old ears, but Drurus didn't seem upset.

"I don't know that song. Who is God? Is that Athena?"

Stephanas listened. "I don't know. I know many gods, but I don't know this god."

"Why would you sing to a god when you're sitting in the stocks?"

"Maybe they think they can make the god happy with songs?" That idea seemed lame, but Stephanas didn't have another. "They are in a hopeless place. They should try to figure out what they did to offend this god after the thrashing they got."

"Do gods always take revenge if you mess up?"

"Our job is to keep the gods happy. We do the right thing, then they do the right thing. Usually. That's an important lesson, son." Stephanas patted Drusus on the head. Why waste a teaching moment?

Drusus pointed at the statue of Athena in the corner of their house. "Did those men made her upset?"

Stephanas didn't care if the prisoners had offended Athena. He only cared if he had done enough so she would protect him. He didn't dare offend Athena.

"I hope this singing doesn't keep the other prisoners awake or they'll be troublesome in the morning." But why should Stephanas care if these men wanted to sing meaningless songs? "Go back to sleep, Drusus."

The boy drifted back to his own bed. Stephanas pulled a blanket over his head and fell asleep.

Stephanas woke to distant rumble, a low growl that rumbled forward like a heavy wagon pulled by a team of horses through the street outside. Darkness still filled the room and Stephanas had no idea the time.

Dust filtered into his face and he blew it from his mouth. Then Stephanas felt the wall beside him bulge, rocking back and forth, while ceiling planks squeaked as though their life was being squeezed from them.

Stephanas heard crashes outside his house as the floor beneath him rose and fell. The wooden stools clattered about, and he squinted, trying to see Athena. Was she angry? Could he yet appease her? He gripped the edge of his cot to keep from being hurled onto the floor. He couldn't offer her incense now. Was it too late?

Then the wall cracked open so that the torch from the jail threw thin light into the room. Stephanas saw the statue pitched forward onto the heaving floor, snapping off its hands and head.

The air was thick with smoke and dirt leaking through the ceiling cracks. Light from a torch burning in the jail flickered wildly and went out.

And then the chaos settled with weak moans, shuddering like a defeated battle field. Shivering like Stephanas himself.

Stephanas leaped to his feet and kicked the stools out of his way as he hurried into the jail. There, one wall had surrendered to the fury and lay as a crumbled slab in the street outside.

What about the prisoners? Stephanas lit a torch, his hands trembling, and stepped through the rubble to shine his light on the dungeon door. It had splintered into pieces and revealed the gaping entrance to the dungeon. He pushed the fallen timbers aside.

If the earthquake had ripped this thick door, what had it done to the stocks and chains in the dungeon? How long had Stephanas clung to his cot as his house pitched in this wave of heaving earth?

THE EARTHQUAKE 69

If he had been a prisoner, he would have clawed his way out of the dungeon. Why would anyone stay unless something trapped them?

Where the air had been dense with the roar of the earthquake, now it was silent. He called into the dungeon, but heard nothing. They were gone. Of course, they were gone. He pulled at his hair and screamed. He had failed.

And in that instant, Stephanas' world collapsed like the surrounding building. He had dreamed of one day sitting with grandchildren on his lap, of riding horses through his estate, of having young soldiers come to him for advice. He'd bribed a few officials to get this position, and it was a good one.

But it was a risky business, and now the dream tumbled around him. The Romans paid their guards and prison officials well. But there was no room for failure, no second chance. A guard who let a prisoner escape had no excuses. They killed him. And his entire household. Wife, children, servants.

This earthquake had stolen Stephanas' future. There was no hope. The Romans had no mercy for botched jobs. They would come soon, arrest him, torture him as an example, and then execute him publicly. Him and his family. How could he allow that? For a moment, he saw Drusus, his wife, his daughters all dragged before crude Roman soldiers. Toyed with. Then killed. He screamed again.

Romans honored failed soldiers who had the good grace to kill themselves, relieving the Romans of that inconvenience. They would leave his family alone in that case. His household would face disgrace but not torture and execution.

What else could he do? There was no future for him now. No hope. Only Roman torture and death.

Stephanas drew his sword.

But then a voice called out. "Stop! We are all here."

A call from the dungeon? An impossible voice giving him an impossible message.

Stephanas sheathed the sword and grabbed a torch, the light trembling with his hand. "Who are you?"

"I am Paul," the man said. "We are all here. No one has escaped."

"Why didn't you escape?" Stephanas held the torch higher, and the light revealed one of the Jews, standing near the opening to the dungeon.

"God had us stay for you." Paul's voice cut through the night air.

Stephanas' knees buckled, and he dropped to the ground. "Do you serve Athena? Did she protect you and me?" Earthquakes came from the gods. Which god had sent this one?

"Athena couldn't do this. You know that." Paul stood in the torch's glow, his head dusty from fallen debris.

Stephanas thought of the broken statue of the goddess lying in his house. Unable to stand. Unable to heal itself. "So what happened?" His pulse pounded in his ears and his stomach tightened. Would these men now jump him and still escape? Would he still face the wrath of the Romans? How could he protect his family?

THE EARTHQUAKE 71

He stood and put his hand on the grip of his sword. Maybe there truly was no hope, no future, after all.

"We serve the true God." Paul sat on the edge of the broken stocks, his face and body caked with dust. "He is the God of grace and love. Have you heard of Jesus?"

The true God? Had they found a god more powerful than Athena? "I know nothing of this Jesus. Or your God."

"This God made the world and everything in it. He gives us a new life."

"I'm in trouble." Stephanas settled onto the top stone step of the dungeon, ignoring the creaking pillars above him. "Can your God help me?"

"Oh, yes, he can help you."

"He can save me from this? From the Romans?"

Paul chuckled. "He already has. Examine the jail. I don't know if God sent the earthquake. But he has saved you. None of the prisoners have left." He glanced over his shoulder into the dark shadows.

Stephanas felt dread lift. At least a little. Maybe men who could sing words of worship in prison had answers he'd never considered.

"I have to be perfect to serve the Romans. And I have to be perfect to serve Athena. No mistakes. Is it the same with your God?" He had no need for another god demanding perfection at every turn.

"You've worked hard to get to your position," Paul said. "I'll bet you were a good Roman officer or you wouldn't be here."

"An excellent officer, plus I offered a good bribe."

Paul rose, but groaned and settled back down. Stephanas rose to fetch water for the prisoners. They drank deeply, each prisoner taking his turn.

"There are always mistakes." Paul wiped his mouth. "Our future is not based on our perfection but on believing in Jesus, God's son. We believe and trust him with the future."

"That's it? Believe him? That sounds cheap. Surely you must do things as well."

"God's not cheap. He's gracious." Paul picked at the dried blood on his arms. Stephanas could see that something was reviving him. Had God done that, too?

Stephanas felt his spirit as parched as the prisoners' thirst, but he longed for more - freedom, truth, and life. Athena offered none of those, and certainly the Romans couldn't. Were those things even possible?

What did these men know?

"You were without hope last night. The Romans would kill you today after flogging you yesterday - and what hope could you have against the Romans?" Stephanas looked up at the jagged ceiling.

"Here's the thing," Paul said. "If God can rescue all of us in an earthquake, what are the Romans to him?"

This Jew had a point. Stephanas rocked his head from side to side in thought. "I want that confidence."

Paul smiled. "Then make him your God."

"Maybe I will. Maybe I have." Darkness still hugged the city as Stephanas rose. "Come with me."

He led the prisoners to the water supply outside his house, where he washed their wounds and scrubbed the dirt from their limbs.

Then Stephanas called his family outside, and they were all baptized. He wanted to seal this new belief. Include them in this new life.

It did not surprise him in the morning when Paul challenged the Romans who came for him. Who could have guessed that he was a Roman citizen? That new information threw the mayor into a panic and the city officials changed their tune to Paul.

"Our God sent Paul to explain new things to us," Stephanas told Drusus the next day. "See how God saved us? He gave us a future."

Drusus nodded. "That's hope, isn't it?"

··········

Digging Deeper

The jailer's story is found in Philippi in Acts 16:22-40. What were Stephanas' hopes and plans before the earthquake struck?

How did the earthquake plunge him into hopelessness?

What did he think would happen in the future?

How did Paul show him new hope in God?

Behind the Scenes
Many retired Roman officers earned land or businesses in Philippi in the first century as a reward for their service to the Roman Empire. Most of the citizens were militantly loyal to Rome.

The city was diverse with people from different provinces and had many temples for various gods. But there was no Jewish synagogue in the city, meaning there weren't even ten Jewish men to establish one.

The false religions of those days demanded precise behavior and sacrifices to appease the gods. The idea of grace or justice or freedom was not part of those religions.

The Singer

"Don't let the darkness blind you, be the light that you are in the presence of God."
—Jesus Apolinaris

"...do not fear them or their words. Don't be afraid even though their threats surround you like nettles and briers and stinging scorpions..."
—Ezekiel 2:3

·······

Stephanas faced a black future—to the point he was ready to end his life. His life plan hadn't worked out as he designed it. But when he cried out for help, he learned God had already put pieces in place to bring new hope to him. I'm certain he became part of the new church that developed in Philippi after Paul's visit.

Our next story follows two young African women from Eritrea who have bright futures ripped away from them unfairly. How will they endure fading dreams and unjust circumstances?

· · · • • • • · · ·

"Hurry, Batha! We're going to miss the opening songs." Senait held the door to their tiny apartment open and waved at her high school friend.

Batha grabbed her bag. "I'm ready. We could miss the first song, you know. Nobody would know."

"Run! I don't want to be late."

Batha lifted her shoulders like she wanted to protest, but Senait grabbed her elbow and pulled her along. They sprinted along the sidewalk in Asmara, the city that held their dreams. They hoped.

Senait heard a rich symphony of musical notes and instruments blending into charming harmony. Maybe that was just the warm-up band. She wanted to hear it all. All the musicians and songs in the city.

Batha slowed. "I can't breathe. Let me rest for a minute."

Senait stepped forward. Three little paces. And then the music stopped.

There were screams. Shouting. A few popping noises.

"Stay here." Senait ran toward the church where the concert was being held. She turned a street corner to see a crowd moving like the rapids of the river near her hometown. People swirled wildly as they tried to escape the courtyard. Pushing. Screaming.

Uniformed officers carrying sticks elbowed their way through the crowd. Some had already found their prey. Men wearing bright orange and blue and yellow silky costumes were in the grip of uniforms. Some uniforms were on each side of a performer, pulling him so fast that he lost his footing. No matter. They kept dragging him.

A woman dressed in long blue robes bounced off Senait and kept running. "Get away!" she shouted as she bolted down the side street.

"What happened?" Senait's question hung in the air.

"They're arresting Christians. Go now. Go."

Senait turned back to the milling courtyard. An officer struck a man, and he dropped into the swirling crowd. The officer grabbed his arm and dragged him to the curb where a line of official vans stood like train cars ready for loading.

After throwing the man into a van as if he was a sack of flour, the officer turned and slowly scanned the crowd. Senait hid by pulling back into the corner. What was happening?

Then Batha appeared at her side and asked the same question.

"We need to return to our apartment," Senait said. "It's ugly here."

••••••••••

Some postage stamps may be bigger than the friends' apartment. They rushed through the door and both sat on the foot of their twin beds. A hot plate and small refrigerator lined the wall beside Batha's bed while their plastic folding table had to be stored beside Senait's bed.

Batha stared at the floor for a long while. And then, "What did you see?"

Senait kept staring at the floor as well. "A wild crowd. And policemen were grabbing people. Throwing them in police units. A woman said the police were arresting Christians."

"We need to get out of the city. Maybe tonight."

"What about your dreams of being a chef? What about my dream of a recording contract? We can't have those if we leave."

"But no one would arrest us back home." Batha stood then and reached for a red tea kettle. "Let me heat some water for tea. We can calm ourselves." Her hands trembled as she worked.

"I remembered something we heard in church." Senait reached to the head of her bed to snag her black-covered Bible. She shuffled through some pages. And then read, "'These trials will show that your faith is genuine. It is being tested as fire tests and purifies gold.' That's from 1 Peter. We're seeing trials."

"I don't know if I want to be purified and tested." Batha grinned then. "But I trust God, too. Maybe not like you, but I do. Really, Senait. But I'd rather have no trials."

"I agree."

The tea kettle blasted a whistle of steam that made both women jump. Clearly, the calming hadn't set in yet.

Batha glanced at Senait. "Put away your Bible. Just in case."

"In case what?"

"They come to arrest us."

"I will not. What kind of Christian would I be if I hid?" Senait thumbed through her Bible again.

"A safer one."

"God gave me this gift to sing. I will stay and give my concert. Wouldn't I be insulting God if I ran away?"

··········

The night of the Senait's concert came, and she sang at a crowded church where music lovers applauded her every song. Her clear voice was like crystal among common clay. The notes floated in the air and then rushed to embrace the ears of her audience. Yellow and red blossoms drifted onto the stage like her melodies.

Open windows and doors ushered in the warm evening air. Aloe and lavender tossed fragrances into the church, weaving among the listeners. As her last song ended, Senait bowed to the audience. The people didn't applaud for a moment, spellbound by the beauty of her songs.

And then the clapping came, rippling through the building with enthusiastic hands. "God bless you!" Senait shouted to her admirers. "God bless you!" they responded.

Batha met Senait backstage after the concert holding a bouquet of purples and reds and blues. "Your songs were beautiful. Wow! Your songs touched the people and I think you really honored God. Plus, I saw that recording agent in the crowd. The one you met last week. You were right!"

After the last person finally exited the church, after many hugs and autographs, Senait and Batha walked toward their apartment. The evening air was cool, with a faint scent of blossoms.

Shadows coated the buildings as they walked. And then the shadows moved. A low growl filled the air and then a new sound: leather slapping against metal. Senait heard a click. This was a gun being cocked. Senait had heard that sound in the courtyard. Then wood popping against skin.

The shadow grew larger as a group of men in crisp gray uniforms circled the two women.

Several slapped wood batons against their palms. One man had a whip, and another held a pistol. The quiet growling rumbled, and then the men raised the batons. One flashed down and struck Senait on the shoulder. Then on her back and head. Were they hitting Batha as well? She turned her head to see Batha on the ground with her arms over her head. Blows kept falling.

Senait lost her footing then and fell. The uniforms closed in with batons and open hands slapping.

"Run, Batha." Senait screamed. "They've come for me." Pain radiated from her arms, her back, her legs.

But Batha didn't leave.

"They warned you," a man shouted. "You've broken the law." The beating stopped. Senait opened an eye. Were they done?

Strong hands gripped her arms and dragged her away.

At what appeared to be a police station, the officers shoved Senait into a tiny room with cold cement walls. No windows.

Where was Batha? Had she escaped?

Senait leaned a hot cheek against the cold bars. She tried to swallow the dryness in her throat. Her hands fluttered and her legs were like old pudding. Could she sit? There was nothing to rest on, and she sank to the cement floor.

She had no time to rest. A muscular man pushed her down a short hall to a room where a man in a gray uniform, his black hair clipped short, sat at a metal table. He drummed his fingers on the table like this was one more inconvenience for a man in the power seat.

"You will die, you know. What you have done is illegal." He pulled back his lips to reveal jagged yellow teeth.

"Singing?" Senait said. "Singing to God? Praying to God? These things are illegal? Why should they be?"

Squat backhanded her. Blood trickled from her lip. "Your church is not registered. Therefore, this concert is illegal." He leaned closer, his breath smelling of beached fish. He raised his eyebrows.

"But I can help. Promise never to do this again. I will release you if you just change your ways. Sign a paper stating that you won't sing in an unregistered church. Simple."

"Never."

His demands and the threats continued through the night. His repetition was as tiring as his squinty eyes and shouts. As the dawn threw some light into the room, Senait dropped her head and arms on the metal table where she sat. Her body ached and her head was swimming. Even had Squat left the door open, she couldn't run a straight line.

He had stepped out for a few minutes and returned, gripping a white mug steaming. Probably coffee. "You're going to Me'etr." Two uniforms grabbed Senait's forearms and pushed a burlap sack over her head. She fell into a vehicle and then felt another thump. Someone joined her.

"Batha?" She had hoped her friend had escaped.

"We're being purified." Batha lisped like many wasps had stung her lips. "Tested but not defeated. God is here."

After a long truck trip, new uniforms tossed the women onto the ground like dry husks after shucking corn. Senait shook her head to dislodge the sack. They were in a desert with the sand stretching from flat horizon to flat horizon. Fences were unnecessary since there was nowhere to escape to. Only more miles of dead desert.

Across the compound were structures. Senait squinted. Already waves of heat were rising from the sand, blurring the landscape. "What are those?"

"Metal shipping containers," Batha whispered.

Each container was twenty feet long. They would find out that eighteen prisoners were packed into each container.. By mid-day, the sun heated the container so that they could boil an egg inside. If they had an egg. Or extra water.

The only window was the size of a paperback book, crudely punched into a wall. Rust and stagnant water collected in a corner.

The prisoners slept inside the containers with barely room for each to lie down. Senait searched for an open area for her and Batha to claim.

"Go to the back." The low voice of a woman hissed at them. Like a snake. Senait looked down at the woman who was also curled into a ball like a snake. "No room here."

There was no path to the back. Senait finally stepped between bodies. A woman yowled like a cat when its tail is stomped on. Had Senait stepped on her? "Sorry."

Some bodies didn't move. The women just rolled slightly, showing no energy to complain. Senait and Batha found a spot to sit and pulled the worn blankets over them. The guards had given each of them a faded green blanket, a ceramic mug, and a bottle of water. What else could they need?

"That woman scares me." Batha beckoned at a form on the floor near them. "She coughs all the time."

"Yes," Senait said. "And the moaning from that one." She beckoned with her head at another lumpy form on the floor.

Batha wrapped her arms around her knees and leaned her chin down. "Do you think anyone knows where we are?"

"Maybe not." Senait tried to draw her thin blanket over her head to block out the groaning, but that didn't help.

"It looks hopeless." Batha wrapped her arms over her head.

"No. God is with us, so we are never without hope."

Senait could hear Batha taking deep breaths. "I forget sometimes. But you're right. How will we get through this unless God is with us?" Batha said.

"Let's keep reminding ourselves of that." Senait looked at the woman who was hacking and coughing. Lying on the ground. Her hair was a mass of knots. No blanket.

Senait leaned across a sleeping body and spread her ratty blanket over the woman's shivering body. "God bless you." The woman wheezed but didn't open her eyes.

Senait and Batha escaped the container every morning as soon as the guards slid the doors open. After waiting in the food line where guards ladled thin beige liquid—maybe long-boiled oatmeal?—into their mugs, the pair walked the compound until the sun's head drove them into the container for shade.

They settled into a routine. Rise, stand in line for the latrine. Stand in line for oatmeal. Walk.

One night, they sat against the wall of the container, its corrugation pressing into their backs. "Remember your concert?" Batha said.

"It was a beautiful night. Until after."

"I had never heard you sing like that before. Your music was so clear. I remember how the flowers smelled. Their scent filled the church. And your songs did, too."

"Sometimes I'd rather forget."

"Because we were arrested?" Batha didn't let Senait answer. "I remember God was there, at your concert. I didn't see it so well then, but I see it now."

"Thank you, Batha. I need to remember that, too. I could feel God with me as I sang. He was touching people through those songs. Now there are just the trials. I wonder when he'll touch people again."

"We'll remember together."

·········

As the weeks went by, Senait noticed the dark hollows under Batha's eyes deepened each day. And Batha lagged when they walked. Stopped to catch her breath often.

Then Batha rejected a morning walk. "I think I'll take a nap today."

"But the air and exercise are good for you."

"Yes, they are." Batha wandered toward their shipping container. Senait circled the container twice before searching for Batha. Sure enough, she was lying on her side in the container, sleeping.

Senait shook her. "Did you eat today?"

"I tried." Batha's voice came in gasps. "I couldn't swallow today. It reeked. I thought I would vomit." Her hands trembled.

When mocking guards ladled the next day's slop, Basha leaned her bony back against Senait's chest and sipped the swill that Senait poured into her mouth from a cracked mug. Batha didn't have the strength to lift the food to her dry lips. As she swallowed, Senait sang to her.

Senait hadn't sung since the concert in Asmara the night they were taken. The dry heat of the desert had tried to steal away her voice, but today Senait opened her mouth. Notes clear as crystal floated into the dead air. The songs from the concert. Songs from church services. Songs from her childhood. They all rose in a melody that reminded Senait of the lavender blossoms at her concert.

Batha slept through most of this concert but another woman, lying close by, raised on her elbow. "You sing with the voice of an angel. I had forgotten about God, but you helped me remember." She touched Senait's foot with her thin fingers.

Soon, Batha spent her days curled into a tight ball on the floor of the shipping container, sweating in the searing heat of the noon sun. Then a day came when Batha couldn't walk to the latrine. Instead, she collapsed on legs like cooked spaghetti. So Senait carried her.

The morning slipped away as they inched their way to the outhouse, but Senait sang as they crept along. Batha cried with each step. "I'm so sorry," she whispered. "I am so tired."

Batha slept most of every day and Senait walked, returning often to check on her. Sometimes Senait could find a little extra water and bring it to Basha.

Often she sang for hours while rubbing Batha's back and shoulders. Other women gathered in the container to listen.

"God is here," Senait sang. "He has never left us." She stroked Batha's feverish forehead. Dehydrated? Could she hear the songs? Was she dying?

Women crowded into the container daily to hear Senait's voice. Four other women carried one woman, who seemed weak as Batha. She lay on the floor close to Senait, her face calm. "You make me so happy, sister," she whispered. "You helped me remember God."

She was gone the next day. Senait asked, but her companions didn't know what had happened either. Only that the guards had taken her away.

New songs about God's love popped into Senait's mind and she mingled those with her other songs. She could sing all day and her voice didn't fade in the heat. Her audience grew. The women listened for hours as she sang.

One day, two guards burst into the container and pushed past the other women. They stood over Betha and checked the identification on her arm. Then they picked her up like a rolled up carpet and marched toward the door of the container.

"What are you doing?" Senait said.

"She's going home."

Senait scrambled to her feet and threw her arms around Betha's slight body. "Let me say goodbye."

She put her lips close to Batha's ear and whispered. "The government doesn't want you to die here. It complicates things. But you will recover at home with good food and rest. God will bring you back to life. Then escape to another country. Leave Eritrea."

Basha's eyes fluttered, and she squeezed Senait's hand. "Remember." Her word faint as a wisp of smoke.

Then she was gone. Senait watched a battered truck roll out of camp, carrying Batha back to her family. Would Senait see her again?

Senait turned to another prisoner, huddled in a tattered green blanket on the floor. The woman wheezed, her thin body shaking. She coughed and reached out a trembling hand.

A new song rose in Senait's heart. She leaned closer to the woman. Grasped her frail hand. "Remember that God loves you, sister. How can I help?"

·········

Digging Deeper

This story illustrates the hopelessness that we all naturally want to avoid. Yet, as Senait learned from 1 Peter, the Early Church suffered similar persecution. We may never be called to this kind of persecution, but there are important lessons to be learned about hopelessness. Why didn't Senait and Batha give in to the guards' demands?

Read 1 Peter 1:6-7, which addresses the suffering of first-century Christians. List the outcomes of faith being tested.

How would those outcomes form a confident anticipation of the future?

Behind the scenes
This story is a composite of stories of imprisoned Eritrean women. Once the Eritrean government determined that there were only four legal faiths in the country (Eritrean Orthodox, Roman Catholic, Sunni Islam, and Evangelical Lutheran Church of Eritrea), officials began a concentrated drive to seize Christians and imprison them.

The Eritrean government Imprisoned many of the Christians in the early 2000s, and their families, to this day, have no news of any charges against them. Some prisoners, like Batha, were sent home because they are very ill. Some have recovered and escaped the country.

But some Christians, attempting to flee, were arrested on the way. No one knows how many have died because of the sparse and cruel conditions.

I based some of this story in *The Nightingale* by Helen Berhane, who describes her imprisonment in Eritrea. Other details came from The Voice of the Martyr website including information about a faithful woman named Twen.

Both Helen and Twen were eventually released, but hundreds of Christians remain imprisoned.

The Money Chapter

"When you stay in faith, continue to trust, and never lose hope out of your darkest moments, you will see blessings rise up."
—Charles F Glassman
"I will not be afraid, for you are close beside me."
—Psalm 23:4b

··········

Senait and Batha remained loyal to God even when their government persecuted them harshly. Hardship did not drive them to hopelessness, as some might expect. Instead, they remained loyal to the Lord despite the cruelty of their own government. They believed God was in their future.

Now we'll meet two young sisters navigating the loss of a marriage plus looming financial impossibilities. They might not be aware of God's work, but can they move forward in hope and steadfastness?

••••••••••

The heavy skies dumped their burden as I drove into the little town, layering rain like Vaseline on my windshield by the time I found the trailer court. As I guided my car onto the dirt driveway, bouncing my way over an archive of old ruts, a sad row of mobile homes blurred in the rain.

What a way to start my vacation.

Ann flung open her front door, sweeping me and some rain into her tiny living room. I dropped my suitcase and gave her a long hug, her bulging tummy poking into me. A strange sensation: my younger sister was pregnant. I hadn't seen her since Christmas and this was a world apart: early June in Missouri, twelve hours from my home.

"So…" I looked down at my suitcase and glanced around the room. Standard '70s paneling that warped and gaped at seams. Faded green curtains. A lumpy brown couch with a particle-board end table. The carpet pattern faded into a trail worn through the threads.

"You're sleeping in here." She waved her hand limply around the living room and dropped onto a recliner older than the house. It groaned.

"OK." I pushed my suitcase closer to the couch and sat down. The couch gave no resistance, and I almost settled onto the floor. My knees didn't bump my ears, so there was that benefit. What a great vacation. "So how's it going?"

This was the lamest of questions when you're sitting in a dented tin box with your pregnant sister who was separated from her husband. I asked it anyway.

Ann shrugged. "I'm still working. I can take a little time off this week while you're here. We can go to a national park one day. I thought about trying for Branson, but that'd be a long day. But it could be fun. There are lots of things to see around here, too." She gave me a quick smile that faded into sadness. More of a weak attempt at a smile, really.

"Do you think it'd help if I talked to Clark?" I liked Clark and maybe he'd listen to the older sister: me.

"After the miscarriage, he said he thought that meant we weren't supposed to be together. When I got pregnant now, I thought he'd be happy. But he says he's done."

So maybe an older sister's talk wouldn't help.

We penciled in some plans for my vacation. But thick rain fell all week. So much for plans.

Above my new friend, the lumpy couch, hung a painting that Ann had created in high school. The scene was alive with red and golden leaves from oak trees that flanked a babbling mountain stream. I knew that if she painted the scene now, it would be shades of gray. My vivacious sister had faded into grief and hopelessness.

Rain canceled any vacation trips. We did splurge for an evening of nachos buried under a jalapeno mountain—enough to make our stomachs hurt. That and an old movie. Making those vacation memories.

Since the rain washed out any outings, Ann went to her job, and I scrubbed walls. Washed dishes. Wiped countertops. Folded laundry. Not as memorable as the jalapenos, but possibly helpful.

And then one evening, she burst into the house with eyes blazing. "I've had enough."

"What—"

"I'm going with you to Colorado."

"What—" I needed to work on my replies.

"I saw him cruising the streets with a bunch of teenagers. He had a cheerleader hanging all over him."

Okay then.

We spent the next day packing, stowing her belongings in my car, and then starting the twelve-hour drive back to Colorado. We'd done road trips before, usually punctuated with laughter and stories. No laughter this trip.

I drove. Ann stared out the window.

The Kansas prairie along I-70 offered no distraction for me, but apparently the miles of grass carpeting rolling hills provided Ann with fascinating study material. She didn't say much.

"It feels weird to come back to Colorado like this," she said as we passed the wooden *Welcome to Colorado* sign. "What future do I have? I still want to fix things with Clark. Both of us made mistakes. We're both to blame."

"You can still work on your marriage if you want." I was full of that kind of helpful advice.

"Where am I going to sleep?" That kind of randomness filled our summer as her mind darted from Clark to a job to the heat.

"Wherever you want."

We arrived at my home in the Colorado summer scorcher days. No rain, though.

Missouri kind of rain never comes to Colorado. A Colorado summer afternoon is like opening the oven to put in a pan of cookies. The blast will curl your eyelashes. In Missouri, the heat clings like adhesive from an old label. I was glad to leave it behind.

In a tidal wave of that summer's emotions, I lingered at the edge. My job was to pay bills and provide a safe home so Ann could heal.

Speaking of paying the bills, I had only quickly punched numbers into a cheap calculator when she decided to come to my house. The final tally wasn't a red under-the-water negative, so surely I could handle these finances.

After all, how much would a pregnant sister add to my monthly bills?

I wish there would have been sound effects to accompany each check I wrote by the tenth of each month, because my monthly salary whooshed away like the sound of a cartoon character being knocked off his feet. Like Wile E. Coyote sailing downward from the towering cliff to the desert floor. Like Goofy screaming, "Yee-hoo-hoo-hoo."

There was the mortgage payment. Yee-hoo. Then the gas card. Yee-hoo-hoo. The utility bill. Yee-hoo-hoo-hoo. Phone. Tithe. Yeeeee-hooo-hooo-hoooo.

After I paid the bills, I stowed the checkbook in my desk drawer and called out to my sister. "Math still works."

"Uh-huh," she said from the living room, which was her way of saying, "I don't want to hear about math."

That didn't stop me from expounding on my financial update. Our family didn't stop for such minor things as disinterest. "Once again, we have money left after paying the bills. Now we can work on the grocery list for the month."

In those days - and this was ancient times when a gallon of gas cost $1.20 and a gallon of milk was $2.26 - we also had a crude little app that could generate a menu for the month and spit out a shopping list.

We could select meals for each day of the month. Moving meals to different days was ok, but there was no fudging on the plan. No eating out. As long as we followed the plan, we didn't have to skip any meals. It was The Menu.

We had $80 for groceries after paying bills and, if we adhered to the plan, we could get through the month. This involved leftovers, too, which were factored into The Menu.

About those leftovers...

Our mother often served beef liver when we were children because she wanted us to have the healthiest and best meals. Whether or not we wanted to as kids, we learned to eat liver cooked Mom's way.

Plus, liver was a cheap protein, so The Menu always included beef liver. So, one month, we'd already had our first meal of liver and had carefully stowed the rest in the refrigerator for a later meal.

One evening, I called out to my sister. "We're eating leftovers. What do you want?" I assumed she knew what was in the fridge.

"Liver."

Hmmm. I was a little surprised, but I stuck the slices of liver in the microwave, punched in a minute on the timer, and then served them up for her. She sat down at the table and stared at an oblong brown chunk on the plate.

I stared, too, because the microwave, in re-heating the slices, had produced little volcano holes all over the top of the liver. It looked like the pockmarks on the surface of the moon.

That shouldn't affect the taste much, I figured.

But my sister leveled two hawk eyes on me. "I said, 'Anything but liver.'"

She wasn't eating any of that volcano liver and it probably messed up our menu for the month. That's how tight our budget was. Leftovers were gold.

Ann worked hard to revive her marriage from a distance that summer. She wrote letters and made phone calls. Apologizing. Pleading. Trying to fan life into a dying marriage.

In early September, we stepped into a new adventure when her labor pains started. I was in the delivery room when my nephew was born, a pink and healthy boy who captured my heart from day one.

We had been home from the hospital only for a few hours when a Sheriff's deputy in full uniform appeared at our front door. He paced a bit in the dim porch light until Ann came to the door.

"Papers for you." He handed a big manila envelope to Ann as though it was fiery hot and would burn her. He was right.

"Divorce papers." Ann sank onto a chair and let the envelope tumble to the floor. "Now what?" Tears came and soon her shoulders shook. "I have no future."

But part of her future began crying from the next room. Ann sighed. Held her breath for a bit, and walked to the crib to pick up her son.

·········

I was the bill payer. When I had run the numbers through my calculator in Missouri, a number came up. I guessed I could pay all the bills every month with $25 left over.

That turned out to be pretty accurate. We tumbled through each month, basically spending nothing extra. One month, we splurged and attended a high school football game. And bought popcorn. That required $14 right there.

My more-experienced self would go back to that naïve young me and say, "Are you crazy? $25 isn't enough margin to get through a month. This will not work."

Trust in God sometimes starts out as naivete. At least it did for us. We went through a full year with almost no extra cash.

Every month, I deposited my paycheck in the bank, and every month, I paid my bills. All of them.

From my current vantage point, that looks impossible.

One time my sister got $100 in the mail. We don't know who sent it, but the money provided her with some cheese and milk.

Sometimes our parents would send a few packages of their farm-raised beef. Happy dance time!

Ann had done photography and darkroom work for a small newspaper in Missouri. But there was no opening in my town for her skills.

So my sister found a part-time job where she could bring my newborn nephew along. He slept while she did office work. She earned enough to buy diapers and a few extras for him. That was good because my $25 wouldn't have bought him many diapers.

To this day, I don't understand how the finances of that year worked. We were busy with life. She tended her newborn. I tried to support her emotional state. We didn't really have time for math.

One evening, after a meal of leftovers and not volcano liver, I leaned back in my chair. "I have a weird story for you."

Ann smirked. "Is it weird because you're telling it?"

"Maybe. Just listen. Our life reminds me of that story in the Old Testament about the flask of oil that never quit. You remember, don't you?"

"A flask of oil?"

"Yeah. I was just reading about the prophet Elisha. There was this poor widow who asked for help."

Ann picked up her son, and he leaned his soft head against her cheek. "This story has a point, right?"

"Don't mine always?"

"Don't make me answer that. You said it was weird."

"OK. So this widow had two sons. She was going bankrupt because her creditors were ready to enslave her sons until they paid the bill."

"That's kinda dumb of the creditors. How do you earn any money if you're a slave?"

"True. But that's how things worked then. Anyway, the widow asked Elisha for help. He asked her what she had, and she said she had some olive oil. So he sent her out to borrow every jar she could find. She kept filling jars with oil and her sons kept going to the neighbors until there weren't any jars left. Then Elisha told her to sell the oil and pay her debts."

"That's a weird story."

"Probably. I thought so, too."

"Does it have a point?"

I got up from the table and carried my plate to the kitchen sink. "The point is: there was enough for the widow. She thought she was about to die because she had no resources. But there was enough."

··········

There was enough for us, too. God did with my bank account what he did with that flask of oil.

I've asked many times, what did he bring out of that time in my life? What did I learn?

Sometimes when we go through hardships, we would do well to remember Romans 8:28: "And we know that God causes everything to together for the good of those who love God and are called according to his purpose for them."

Something else I've learned is to include Romans 8:29, that adds, "...[God] called [his people] to become like his Son...."

His Son, Jesus, had hardship in his life. Jesus suffered and God worked through that sacrifice to achieve what God wanted to achieve. Jesus didn't have a life of easy leisure.

So how did that apply to my life?

Life often includes challenges.

The Menu included hardships, too. Besides volcano liver. Well, volcano liver might have been an exceptional hardship, but there were others.

Just writing checks every month to keep the lights on, the gas flowing, the tithe covered required some trust. Because that bank account was thin as Colorado roses blooming in January.

Looking back, I recognize amazing things. I didn't have a high-paying job, but I never was at risk of losing it. My church family wrapped their arms around my sister, and I suspect some of the anonymous gifts came from them.

My car never broke down. The furnace kept pouring out heat. We didn't have to replace clothes - except for the little guy and there were always larger clothes for him when he needed them. I'm not sure where they came from.

I paid my bills every month, and we had enough.

In that hard time, God came through like a fireman bursting through the smoke into a flaming house.

God provided, and I don't know how.

I still can calculate a budget, so I know that the plan to support my sister really was like Wile E. Coyote's schemes. Failure hovered at the edges of our path, ready to flatten us without notice.

The financial squeeze changed me: I have never been worried about finances since. I still trust God to provide. Like Elisha's flask of oil, we don't always know how he works. He just does.

It's easy to praise God when we have plenty, when the paycheck is hefty and our debts are all manageable.

When we don't need to trust him.

But when pain kicks out our feet and we crash to the ground, when all our strength has drained away, trust can be difficult.

But if we pay attention, there's strength, too. Not in us, but in God.

For me, that year of financial shortness and yet amazing plenty taught me that God will provide.

God makes a pledge: "I will never leave you or abandon you." (Heb. 13:5 NLT) Never is a strong word. But if we can grasp it, we can walk into the future.

That is hope.

··•••·•···

Digging in:
Read Hebrews 13:5. Although I didn't quote all of Hebrews 13:5, it includes an appropriate caution regarding money. How does it help us to find satisfaction with what we have?

Read Romans 8:28-29. How do those verses give you an understanding of hard times? What can you learn?

Behind the scenes
Although the substance of this story regarding my sister and me is true, I have changed details for anonymity and clarity. Our parents were deeply

involved in the trip to Missouri and in transporting Ann back to Colorado. I combined them into one character to simplify the story. They were both very generous, but they didn't contribute much to our financial plan that year. I think God wanted us to learn to trust him, not their checkbook.

Ann's son was born healthy, and I witnessed his birth. I also experienced a loving year with the little guy as an infant and, later, as a toddler who came running to me when I got home from work, begging for a trip to the park. The house was quiet and cold when Ann moved to our parents' town a year later to attend the community college there.

Before long, she met a young man she had gone to high school with. They married and had two more sons together. They remain married to this day.

Five years after Ann moved out, I married a widower with four children and we had two more children together, too. A family filled my once-empty home. And we have enough.

Mechanics

"We find God in the midst of the trauma we face, not removed from it. His holiness means being involved. He doesn't always heal us as quickly as we'd like, but he never turns his back on us no matter what."
—Patrick Regan

Give thanks to the Lord, for he is good! His faithful love endures forever.
—Psalm 118:1

··•••·•••··

Financial uncertainty can snatch joy and hope from our lives. Our last story examined how God can work in mysterious ways in finances, trading despair for hope in what looked like impossible circumstances.

When a man faces a gut-wrenching medical diagnosis, is his faith in God enough? A young friend asks the same questions.

· · · · •· • · · ·

The oily nut screeched in protest as a giant wrench gripped the hardware and steadily turned it. Strong, greasy hands grasped the wrench and, when the nut finally wound its way into his hand, Tony leaned back. Step one done.

"Hey, Tony, I got a question for you."

Tony looked up from the floor where he sat, half enclosed by the giant tractor, and saw Elliot casting a shadow over his work. "About your tractor?"

"I need a little help." Elliot shifted his weight from one foot to the other. The lifeblood of the tractors they were repairing stained his uniform, like Tony's, with dusky oil. "I met this guy the other day, and he says he knows you."

"Could be." Tony got to his feet and wiped his hands. "Let's take a break, and I'll see if I can defend myself."

The two mechanics ambled into their company's break room, a long room with a line of chairs along two walls, and old linoleum covering the floor. Each man filled a styrofoam cup with steaming coffee. Tony sank into an orange plastic chair, and Elliot plopped down across from him, stretching his long legs out. "Remember when I had to get some stitches at the hospital?"

Elliot held up his hand where a jagged red line crossed the meat of his thumb. Tractor grease had buffed the stitches, but Elliot was young. It'd heal.

"Sure." Tony sipped his coffee. Hot.

"There was a guy there. Real friendly sort. He was talking to everybody who came through. He asked me a bunch of questions about me and then he laughed. Said he used to work here. Said he knew you."

Aha. Tony nodded calmly. "Tall, good-looking guy with a big grin? Did he tell jokes, too?"

"He even did a John Wayne imitation," Elliot said. "I was late getting back to work. Don't tell the boss, but I sat down and listened to him."

"Sounds like Bryan."

"What's his story?"

"He's lived around here all his life. Big football star in high school. And a great singing voice. He was the lead in the high school musical." Tony chuckled. "I'll bet they picked the musical because of Bryan. It was…. Let me think. What was the name of that thing? It needed a guy who could do an Elvis imitation with a booming voice."

"*Bye, Bye, Birdie.*"

Elliot was more cultured than Tony realized. "How'd you know that?"

"Our school did it one year. But we didn't have a good lead. Ours was a skinny little guy who sang dishwater tenor. You know. His voice reached clear out to the second row. It was a pretty sorry performance, but we were a little school, so whatcha going to do?"

"Bryan was perfect for the role." Tony swirled his coffee cup. By the time the steaming coffee cooled, it'd be time to get back to work. Why did it get so hot? "He had a big booming voice."

"He ever sing when he worked here?"

"Nah. He was good with the customers, but I doubt they wanted to be serenaded." Tony carefully sipped his coffee and looked around the break room. "Nobody brought donuts?"

"Not today."

"Back to work, then." They both ambled back into the big shop where a row of tractors stood in different stages of undress. The rumble of power tools filled the air.

A few days later, Elliot pulled Tony aside again. "I gotta ask you some more about Bryan."

Tony glanced at his tractor, where he was ready to add an oil filter. "What's up?"

"He's at the hospital every day."

"And how do you know that?" Tony wanted to wipe the grease off Elliot's face, but it didn't really matter much.

They were mostly holed up in the big shop, and their customers were often as dirty as they were. Nobody cared about stray grease. That big blotch across his cheek looked like Aruba. Classy.

Elliot shifted his weight from one foot to the other. "I wanted to talk to him, so I snuck in. He told me he's there every day. And he invited me anytime."

"So you went back again? To listen?"

Elliot nodded. "He told me some of his history. He said he used to be pretty wild partier." Elliot cleared his throat. "Like me." His chuckle was more sheepish than humorous, though.

Tony ignored Elliot's admission. "I've heard some stories. By the time he worked here, he'd found Jesus. He was pretty dedicated by that point. But, boy, he knew how to tell a joke."

"Still does." Elliot held a screwdriver in one hand and began tapping it on the wheel of a disembodied tractor. "So, why's he at the hospital every day?"

"Careful, you don't poke a hole in that tire. They are expensive."

Elliot looked down at the tire and the screwdriver. "Oh." He stuffed the screwdriver in his back pocket. Not about to do any work for a little while.

"Did he talk to you about Jesus?" Tony glanced down at the oil dripping into a pan on the floor. It was about time to install the filter, but he waited for Elliot.

"Yeah." Elliot looked up at the ceiling.

Tony let the words hang in the air. There were just a couple of sparrows in the rafters. Nothing much to study. Except questions. When Eliot was ready, he'd ask.

Elliot didn't speak for a little while, and Tony turned the oil filter in his hand, ready to screw it in place.

Then Elliot drew a deep breath. "He said he'd gone to Bible college. And he's been a youth Bible camp director. Who does those things? Is he a weird religious guy?"

Tony laughed. "That's all he told you?"

"Yeah. Is he some hospital missionary or something?"

Elliot was leaning on Tony's tractor. Not getting any work done. Tony didn't point out the line of dismantled tractors standing by for new parts. They could wait.

Tony pulled himself off the cement floor. "Not really. That's not why he's there. I guess he could have told you more. He loves to serve God. Bryan was in charge of a big youth group in town. He's baptized people. Sometimes he preaches. He loves people, and he loves God."

"Yeah." Elliot pulled the screwdriver out of his pocket so he could study it. Like he hadn't seen that stained green handle before. "He's just different. I mean, he was like me but now he's different. I don't know. I oughta get back to work."

"Okay." Tony dropped onto his floor creeper and rolled under the tractor he was working on. Time to get that filter on.

·········

A week passed, and then Elliot came barreling across the shop with renewed purpose. "I found Bryan on Facebook."

"Did you?" Tony crawled to his feet from under a red tractor and brushed off his dusty knees. "Why were you looking?"

Elliot scowled. "I'm trying to figure him out. I know about people who party hard, but I don't know anybody like him. He listens to me. Tells me stories. I don't understand this guy."

Tony raised his eyebrows. "You thought wild partiers never changed?"

"Well, yeah. Maybe. I don't know. I guess I didn't think much about the future. About changing. But he's got kids. Grandkids. And he loves his wife. He had photos of all of them."

"Uh-huh." Tony waited. Elliot slid his hands over an oily wrench. Up and down the handle of the wrench.

"I don't like something I found."

"Oh?"

"He's a great guy, Tony." Elliot's voice squeaked like a kid introducing his parents to his teacher. Strained and awkward. "He's done a lot of good things for people."

"You found the post, didn't you?"

"Yeah." Elliot drew in a long breath. "I saw. He's got Lou Gehrig's disease." He clamped his jaws together and then scowled. "It's not fair, Tony. How could God do that to him? Even I can see all he's done for God."

"Did you ask Bryan?"

"Not yet. I just started reading his posts. He's been busy."

"He started a new ministry, didn't he?"

"I'd be mad at God. But has this thing. ALS Ministry. He's writing encouragement for other people.

He ought to be feeling sorry for himself. How can he post stuff for everybody else?"

"Like what?"

Elliot leaned against a small white tractor, which was dustier than he was, and crossed his arms. "He has this F10 ministry. Ever heard of that? He's praying for his kids and grandkids and great-grandkids. That's not right. He wants to pray for all those people—his family—and he wants other people to do the same thing."

"What's not right about that?"

"The whole disease thing. It's not fair. Why is he worried about his family? Why aren't they worried about him?"

Tony tossed a wrench into his tall tool box drawer and heard the metal clang with other wrenches. "They are. They visit him all the time. They're doing a lot for him."

"Why does he pray for them? Why doesn't he just sit and cry? That's what I'd do. Well, I'd just drink all the time. Stay drunk. That's what I'd do. But he prays for his family?"

"I've tried that, too. Praying for my family."

"You have? What'd you think of it?" Elliot's eyes narrowed then. "You ain't sick, are you? Like Bryan?"

Tony laughed. "Just the usual crazy in the head." He drew a deep breath of air, which smelled somewhat burnt and oily. One of his favorite smells. "It's pretty easy to get so busy we forget about our families. But Bryan helped me to remember my kids."

"You pray? Because of Bryan?"

"Hand me that open-end wrench. I can tighten these bolts while we talk."

"Three-quarters?"

"Yeah."

Elliot reached with the tool. "I ain't got kids. No wife, either. What am I supposed to do?"

Tony put his hand out and felt the wrench plop in his palm. "What do you think Bryan would suggest?"

"Not sure. Pray for somebody else?" Elliot nodded his head. "Like my drinking buddies."

Tony slid the wrench onto a bolt head. "I think Bryan would approve of that."

"So how did this ALS happen to him, anyway? Is it contagious?"

"About a year ago, he started dropping things. He was up on a big combine and he was dropping his wrench."

"I've done that," Elliot said.

"Not that many times. Bryan couldn't figure out what was going on. But he's like us. He didn't pay much attention. Just kept working. Then he fell from the combine."

"That's a ways."

"Yep. That was another odd thing. Still, he wasn't much concerned, but then his back started hurting a lot."

"He knew then?"

Tony finished tightening the bank of bolts and straightened up, rubbing his back. Ironic. "No. He'd played football and been a rodeo guy. He was a big muscular guy who lifted too much heavy stuff. You'd expect a bad back."

"So, when did he figure it out?"

"Doctors found it when he finally went in to check on things. They couldn't figure it out for a while, but it's for sure. He has another year or so."

"Oh, man," Elliot pulled off his oily cap and rubbed a dirty hand through his thick hair. Put the cap back on. "It's not fair. I like him, Tony. He's like me, only he's not. He makes me think."

Just then, their manager called over the intercom. "Hey, the Johnsons are coming in this afternoon. Is their tractor done?" The two mechanics scurried back to their projects.

··········

At a coffee break a week later, Elliot waved his phone at Tony. "A new Facebook post. Bryan has another plan in his ALS Ministry."

Tony bit into a cream-filled pastry. Somebody had fetched a box of donuts, and he was hungry. "Yeah?" Today the coffee was just the right temperature. Add a donut and this was a perfect break time.

"Here's what he wrote: 'As I get weaker in my ALS Ministry, I've been trying to think ahead a bit about what to do when I have the choice to feel sorry for myself.' Oh, man, this is getting to me." Elliot studied his phone for a long time and then drew in a breath. "Why shouldn't he feel sorry for himself? I would."

Tony nodded. "It's hard."

Elliot ran his thumb down the phone's display. Reading. "So here's Bryan's plan. He talked with his kids and grandkids. Listen to this: 'We are trying to set up a plan to have them call each day and read me a chapter of scripture and then close in prayer.'"

"Sounds like Bryan." Tony wiped some donut creme off his chin.

"Wow, that would have changed me if my grandpa—even my dad—ever thought of that. And get this. He says, 'If this would be something that work for you, don't wait until you have a disease to try it out.... Just saying.'"

"That'd be something, huh? People will remember him for those ideas." Tony bit into his donut, followed by the hot coffee. Ah, a great snack. "Did you see his M&M days?"

"No. What are those?"

"Stands for Memorizing Mondays. Spend 30 minutes memorizing a Bible verse. Then get a bag of M&Ms downtown."

Elliot laughed. "That sounds like Bryan."

Tony stretched out his legs, his jeans dusty from the morning's work. "I liked the post about his grandma's funeral. He said that there were tears as they talked about Grandma, but then the little grandkids got in the way of the tears. I remember what he said: 'Life was all around us. Grandma was a believer, too, and that made me very happy. Four generations down from Grandma were all believers. Pretty cool thing to see.'"

Elliot nodded. "And I like how he signs his posts: 'Bryan, 1963 - God only knows.' That's tough. It looks like he's okay with it, though." He sighed. "I still don't think it's fair. Why doesn't he blame God? I—"

"I know. You would." Tony crumpled his napkin and tossed it in the trash. "He still reminds you of you?"

"Maybe. I want to understand him. How can he go on? That looks really hopeless to me. I know people with fewer problems than him who get all depressed. Why isn't he depressed?"

"Keep looking," Tony said. "See what he posts. Keep asking questions. Got a believer in your life?"

Elliot stared at Tony. "You. I think."

"Oh. Sure. Yeah." Tony stood and then plopped back into a plastic chair. "Bryan talks about how hard it is to think about the future when you have ALS. And then he goes and quotes a verse, like from Matthew. 'Do not worry about tomorrow...' He spends all day with the Lord and he talks about how God cares for him."

Elliot crushed the styrofoam cup he held in his hand. "But it looks like God doesn't care for him because he got ALS. Couldn't God have prevented that?"

Tony sighed. "We all wonder that. Things happen. I sure don't know why Bryan got ALS. But notice what God is doing in Bryan. He trusts God even more than he used to. And..." Tony scowled, thinking. "And have you seen what an audience he has? People like you never knew him before. But now you're listening to him and wondering about God. Bet that wasn't happening before."

"So God did this to him so he could tell others about how good God is?"

"I just meant that Bryan gets to know God even better and we get to go along for the ride. Bryan doesn't want to feel sorry for himself."

Elliot kicked at a tiny speck of dirt on the floor. "People feel sorry for themselves for a lot less than what Bryan is going through. My drinking buddies, for example."

"Exactly. Bryan is learning how much God loves him. He's paying attention right."

Elliot nodded. "ALS looks pretty hopeless to me. But Bryan looks at the future different." He tossed his coffee cup across the room into the trash. "He makes me think about my future more. Maybe how I want God in my future. I think that's a good thing, huh?"

"Bryan would be proud of you."

••••••••••

Digging deeper

Read Matthew 6:34. Bryan quotes that verse in a Facebook post. How could that verse help you with your daily difficulties?

Read 1 Peter 5:7, which also talks about our hardships and difficulties. How can you apply that passage to your life?

Behind the Scenes

Although Tony and Elliot are fictional characters, everything I wrote about Bryan is accurate. He is now an icon in his community as he journeys through ALS. He has used his Facebook feed to encourage people in their faith walk as he shares his.

In addition to his ALS Ministry and his M&M Ministry, Bryan encourages his friends and family to make the most of each day. He reminds them the time is short and to do the things they should do, while they still can. Bryan is doing that in his own life. He is leaving a tremendous faith legacy because he trust in God and trusts God for his future, and the future of his loved ones.

How does he face each day without despair? How does he find hope for another day? For Bryan, it's because he is confident in God's actions. He takes on each day trusting God. He has inspired many others with his determined hope in God.

Update: Bryan died on January 2023 with his family at his side. He never lost his faith in God or his hope in eternity.

Defeating The Dragon

"The only way you're going to reach places you've never gone is if you trust God's direction to do things you've never done."
—Germany Kent
"Don't be afraid. Take courage! I am here!"
—Jesus in Mark 6:50b

··········

Bryan has challenged many to examine their own relationship with the Lord and through his words, God has touched many lives with hope and future.

God also declares us to be worthy, even when our circumstances tell us we are worthless. When that truth becomes genuine for us, we will walk into the future knowing we have value to the Creator of the universe.

Some create their own hopelessness by their choices and then, when the bottom leers at them like a ravenous dragon, they long for rescue. A young woman caught in her own fear and despair begins a search for hope. Join her as she hunts for truth and life.

••••••••••

Today it was finding a baby sock that brought the rain forest of tears. Yesterday, Judy cried because the heel of bread was green with mold, leaving her nothing to eat.

She slid her hand down the rusty metal on the inside of the battered van that served as their home. Tears poured like a Seattle shower.

"What's up?" Donny stuck his head into the van door. "You hurt?"

"I found one.... of Jack's... his baby socks." Judy held up the tiny stocking, stained with dirt from the van floor. "The... the case worker... missed it." Words are hard in a monsoon.

Donny shrugged. He stumbled as he stepped back. His eyes were unfocused and swimming, his cheeks red. He'd found some drugs.

"I need something, too." Judy crawled out of the van, dropping the sock. She held out her hand and the black dragon roared like it did every day. Calling her closer.

DEFEATING THE DRAGON 121

Her body ached. Her hands shivered, and voices in her head shrieked like people on a roller coaster. Would she have her children? Ever?

The dragon's teeth punched into her heart.

She held out her hand. Donny dug the baggie out of his jeans pocket and dropped it in her hand.

Then the dragon quieted.

For now.

The roar cooled.

For now.

"I can't deal with this." She settled on the cement curb beside their van. Nobody walked past, and she drew a deep breath. Her heart was pounding. Drugs? Anxiety? Did it matter?

"We have lost all the kids. There's a case file on each one. We have a kid and then we lose them. I can't deal with this."

"Yeah." Donny offered no solutions.

"When do we see the caseworker again?"

"I dunno. Thursday?"

Judy crawled back into the van. She knew there was an appointment card somewhere, but she couldn't remember where. She couldn't remember much right now, thanks to the drugs, but she still remembered her kids. "No! It's tomorrow. We have to get to the office."

"We'll get there. The van runs good." Donny's words slurred.

Judy's eyes drooped. Sleep—lovely sleep—was pulling her into safety. Sleep and drugs. Slipping into a safe place. Where all was quiet and all were safe.

But the next day came. The snarling dragon returned with a vile roar.

What time was the meeting? Judy found a hairbrush in the front seat of the van and tried to untangle her hair. Then she pulled at her clothes. Rumpled. She began pressing them with her hands to smooth the wrinkles.

Donny stuck his head into the van. "What time is our appointment again?"

How could he forget?

They drove to the office and parked in a big parking area. Apparently a lot of people needed social workers.

Brown couches lined the walls of the waiting room, circling a large coffee table with a blanket of magazines. The receptionist checked their names off her clipboard and then ignored them.

Both Donny and Judy had dozed off before Lila, the caseworker, called them in. Judy tried to toss off the drowsiness as they trailed down the hall, past several office doors, and dropped with a thud onto a metal chair.

Lila sat behind a metal desk with a phone to her left side and a ski slope of tan folders on her right. She thumbed through the tabs and pulled out a thick folder. Glanced at the first page. Looked up at Judy and Donny with bored eyes that did this ten times a day.

"So, either of you find a job?" she said. "How about a place to live?"

"We are looking. It's really hard." Judy focused on the shelves behind Lila, also piled high with folders. How many other families were in hopeless straits?

Lila made some notes on a sheet of paper. "It's about impossible without a job. So, your kids are in foster care. You know that, right?"

"Can we visit them?" Could Jack crawl by now? She hadn't been there to see. Was someone reading stories to Elsa? Did the foster people know that Mikey hated blueberries?

"We can arrange monitored meetings. But you need to get off the drugs. Get a place to live. What are you doing to get off the drugs?"

Judy felt the tears coming. She blinked hard. This wasn't the place to cry.

And why didn't Lila realize she needed the drugs? How could she deal with this deadening pain while sober?

"I guess I'm self-medicating." Judy leaned back into the chair, feeling its cold metal against her back. Her voice trembled and tears slid down her cheeks. "Who could… could deal with this… with this while sober?"

"Your kids have to go through this sober." Lila leaned forward and tapped her pen on the paper. "So why can't you?"

What an idea. Why couldn't she? The idea echoed in Judy's mind and then broke through her fog like a shrill shout in a library. The kids worked through foster care every day. What did the kids at school say to them? How did they feel?

Judy hadn't thought of their suffering.

And they couldn't self-medicate.

The dragon roared again in Judy's head, and she leaned away. The dragon growled, flashing sharp dripping teeth. Ready to consume her. Ready to devour her family.

"Another thing." Lila wasn't part of the dragon vision. She had data. Not much imagination. "We are looking for someone to adopt the kids. Or at least the youngest ones."

That couldn't happen. Someone else raise her kids?

Judy left the meeting determined to whip the dragon. She would kick the drugs and get her kids back. She'd bring them home. Just a little self-discipline, right?

The dragon loomed in front of her. Growling. Snapping at her shaky resolve. Crouching, ready to rip courage from her fingertips and toss it in the air. Smash it to pieces.

·········

Judy had no time to map out her new plan of self-disciple. Donny got arrested and sentenced to three months in jail.

Now Judy was alone, with no money. No job. No family. At least the van was paid for.

Their friend Andy poked his head in the van one day. "How's Donny doing?"

"He's in jail. He's getting fed, and it's warm in there." Judy felt the tears coming again. She was like the Pacific Northwest, a deluge of tears flowing daily. Her mind was gray, too, like a Seattle sky. Hopeless. No future for her family. "What am I going to do? I have nothing to eat."

"Well, Donny's guy is looking for someone to sell for him. You'd get some money for food. Maybe even new clothes."

"That scares me, Andy. "

Andy shrugged. "Easy money."

"I'll think about it." But the fears that were slapping her around couldn't hide one fact: she was losing her children. She was a mother. She didn't have any other talents.

What job could she find? None. She had nothing else to offer to an employer. She could imagine writing on a job application: *Skills: mother*. That wouldn't impress anybody.

Losing the children ripped away her only purpose. She had to get them back.

But that couldn't happen if she starved. The black dragon hissed a fiery breath that began melting her plans. Great. Now that dragon, which was her stupid life, was destroying what she wanted.

What choice did she have? Her future was hopeless.

So she dealt drugs.

When she was awake, Judy cried. Pacific Northwest weather every day with her tears. Regret. Pain. Failure.

At the next meeting with Lila, Judy heard the warning again. "There's no way you'll find a place to live or find a good job in time. You will lose your parental rights."

"Are you telling me that our case is hopeless?"

"Pretty much."

Judy went back to the van. No more kids. No more life. No more future. Hopeless.

··········

By the time they released Donny from jail, he was clean and sober.

And with new faith. "God can do this," he told her. But Judy couldn't see a way out of dragon's flames.

Soon, Donny found a job. This was the first step in trying to rebuild their lives.

"We need to find a place to live." Judy had already been searching for every lead she could uncover. A home for their children. Driving up and down streets looking for houses without curtains. Maybe they were vacant. "That's our chance."

"Well, we don't have enough money to get a place. Landlords always want first month's rent and a deposit," Donny said. "We don't have that."

"You keep going to work." Judy held up a newspaper. "I'll keep looking."

The drugs dropped to second place to the house hunt. Judy had to be clean to talk to landlords.

During the day, she'd contact landlords while Donny went to work.

"How'd the house hunt go today?" Donny was home from a day's work and upbeat about the future. By this point, they were sleeping on the couch of a cousin's apartment. Better than the van, at least.

"Horrible." Judy felt the all-too-familiar tears gushing out. "Either the rent was too high or they'd just rented it. And we can't afford anything." Her vision of Jack and Mikey and Elsa faded day by day. Like a train leaving without her. Her Seattle sky opened up again and tears flowed. "It's hopeless."

"God can do this." Confidence flowed from Donny. Faith? Good for him if he'd found comfort, but where was the evidence that God was doing anything?

Judy lived in the swamp of misery. How could she lift one foot from the sludge that gripped her? When Donny went to work, she cried all day. Tears washed across her face and dug deep into her soul. What more could she do?

She decided to try Donny's new approach. Try this God-thing.

"God," she said, "I can't do this anymore. This is too hard. There are no options left." Was he listening? Was he even there? She didn't know how to pray. Maybe he was punishing her instead of listening to her. How would she know?

An idea came. A bulb igniting in a dark closet, almost. Someone needed to pray *for* her. Who? Donny was at work. Who else did she know?

Maybe somebody at a church knew how to pray.

Judy didn't know anyone at a church, so she made her way to the public library. That should be an information hub, right?

Making her way through the stacks of books and magazines, she found the phone books. Tattered books lined up on a shelf.

She laid the first book on a table and ran her finger down the page. There. Churches. She began dialing phone numbers, starting with the top of list and working her way down the page. No one answered.

More tears came. She ought to be dry as the Sahara by now, drained of tears.

She covered her face with her hands, feeling the hot tears trickle through her fingers. Her face was fiery, and the room seemed eery. Library-silent. Condemning her.

The phone book fell to the floor, but she sat still, letting the tears flow. Was this the end, then? Even God couldn't help her?

"Are you kidding me? There's nobody who could pray for me?" Judy tapped her fist on the table. Steady. As though if she stopped banging her fist, she could never go down this path again. She'd be done.

"Can I help you?" A quiet voice pierced her fog.

Judy opened her eyes. The woman wore muted colors and a warm face. And a name tag. *Margaret*. A librarian.

"I can't find anybody. Someone needs to pray with me. I can't find anybody." The words tumbled out in a hot gush. "The churches aren't open. Nobody's answering their phone. I don't know what to do."

DEFEATING THE DRAGON 129

The librarian searched her face. Then studied the window in thought. "Walk downtown. There's a woman that works in a business there. Ask for Brenda."

Judy hesitated. "Is this gonna be weird?" This librarian was asking her to walk into a business, request someone she didn't know, and see what happened.

The librarian shrugged. "I've heard things."

Judy drew in a hot breath. She didn't know this lady, and she didn't know what she was looking for.

"Thanks." She rose from her chair and walked like a zombie outside the library. Would she go? "I need this. I need it." The line of trees outside the library appeared sympathetic, and she spoke to them. "I'm driving myself insane. You know what I mean? I'm crying and crying. I need to do this."

The trees seemed to agree.

Judy walked downtown and pushed open the glass door of the store. No customers. The door whooshed closed behind her.

She stayed in the entry, ready to bolt. How long would it take to pull open the glass door and run? She could be gone before this woman saw her.

But how could she explain this to the library trees? She'd come this far, so she walked a little further into the store.

Then a woman called from the back. "Can I help you?"

The tears had finally shut down Judy's throat. No words came out.

The woman came closer. So calm. "What do you need?"

"I... I need... I need prayer." The tears found a new level and flowed vigorously. "Are you Brenda?"

The woman was middle age with short salt-and-pepper hair. She crossed the distance in a few long steps and wrapped her arms around Judy. "I'm Brenda."

She led Judy to a back room. Boxes of unopened inventory sat on the floor, but Brenda pulled a chair out of the rubble. "Sit here." And then she prayed while Judy cried. "Lord Jesus, you know this precious child. You know the pain in her heart. Begin a healing process."

Brenda prayed. Judy cried. They had a rhythm of prayer and tears.

After two hours, Judy dried her eyes. She stood up and gave Brenda another hug.

"Are you better?"

"I am brand new." Judy felt energy pulsing through her mind. The fog was gone. No sounds from the dragon. No black hole. "I have a new life. I can feel it."

"We called that being born again. You belong to God now."

・・・・●●●●・・

Judy hurried home. Donny had to hear this. When he strolled in the front door after he'd finished his job for the day, he saw her face. "What happened today?" He clasped her hands and led her to his cousin's couch. They sat together, knees touching.

Judy described the day. Even the library trees. "We're going to get the kids back. I know what the lawyer said." She held up her hand as Donny tried to interrupt. "I know he said there was no chance anymore." A wide smile lit her face. "Everything is going to be different."

At their next meeting with Lila, Judy explained the situation. They had a job, and they had a place to live.

"The judge won't buy this," Lila said. "No way. It's been two years since you lost the kids. I don't even understand why the adoptions haven't already happened."

"God was just waiting for us to trust him." Judy didn't need the caseworker's understanding anymore. "I know we'll get the kids back."

Judy and Donny left the office with Lila still shaking her head as she shuffled through their case folder.

They cruised the streets in the evenings, looking for empty houses. They called realtors and searched for any connection who could help them. Finding a house was the key to restoring their family.

And they prayed for a house.

They zeroed in on an empty house. Tiny. The owner didn't want to rent it. But the lure of monthly rent finally convinced him to let them move in.

"It's microscopic," Donny said.

"Yep. But we don't have furniture, anyway. A one-bedroom house will be a challenge with the kids, but we'll manage."

The next surprise was that Lila allowed the children to return to Judy and Donny.

With Elsa and Mikey and Jack squeezed into their house and their hearts, Judy had a new goal. "I need to figure out what I did wrong. God must have had a good reason to put us through this."

"You're trying to keep control." Donny held plates of food for the kids. For meals, they'd all sit on the old blue couch that Brenda had given them. Judy pulled off the pillow and blanket that made the couch a bed. "Let go of that control. God's not punishing you. He just rescued us."

Judy considered that for a time. When the tiny house turned out to have bedbugs, they discarded all their things so that they could move into a two-bedroom trailer house.

Donny found a better job about that time and the whole family began attending a church together. They made many Christian friends.

When friends from their church moved out of town, they offered their house to Donny and Judy and the kids. It had three bedrooms, a dining room, and new kitchen appliances.

"God is taking care of us," Judy told Donny. "This isn't what I expected, but it's pretty amazing."

"So, do you have hope now?"

"I'm working on it. I'm still not sure what hope looks like." Judy began talking to her pastor. Her friends. And a new veil lifted.

"I'm starting to understand," she told Donny. "God is helping me understand. Hope happens during hardship."

"We've had some hardship."

"But the biggest thing I've learned is that hope is a gift. Since Brenda prayed for me, I've never been in a place of hopelessness. Even when we couldn't find a place to live."

··········

After his day at work, Donny strode into the kitchen, past the built-in dishwasher and stainless steel sink, to the gleaming stove where Judy stood. "This is a pretty amazing place that God gave us."

"God has given us more than a house. We have hope." Judy stirred the hamburger in a pan on the stove. The kitchen smelled of freshly baked cookies and boiling potatoes. "Sometimes hope is as simple as 'Oh, I'm almost out of gas but God will get me home.' It's confidence." She pulled open the oven door and drew out the sheet of cookies. The kids would be home soon. And they were always hungry. "I know that God's got me. Even when I'm dumb. He's got me."

Donny stuck a fork into the browning meat. "You're not dumb." He bit the meat off the fork. "Yum."

Judy pushed his arm. "Quit snitching." But then she kissed him. "God is not vengeful. I thought he was. The devil says, 'Yes, he is.' We can't stay pure enough. If our hope depends on never making a mistake, we won't have hope. If anybody deserves to be ignored by God, it's us. But he didn't. Hope means that God's got me."

Donny wrapped his arms around her. "God's got our whole family. Here's to hope."

・・・●●・●●・・・

Digging Deeper:
Describe a time when you wondered if God was being vengeful to you. How did you work through that?

Judy described hope as confidence in God. Do you agree with her? Describe a time when you experienced this confidence in God.

Judy also discovered that hope is a gift. Have you also found that to be true in your difficulties?

Behind the scenes:

I changed names and circumstances, but this story is based on interviews with Judy herself as she recounted how addictions took her to places she never wanted to go. She and her husband have been sober for several years now. Their family is intact and their faith in God is vibrant.

The Wall

No relationship is all sunshine, but two people can share one umbrella and survive the storm together.
—Unknown

"But then I will win her back once again. I will lead her into the desert and speak tenderly to her there."
—Hosea 2:14

· · · • • · • • · ·

Addiction became a snarling dragon for Judy, stealing away her children and squeezing out many tears. Future? There was no future with the dragon. But Judy found a way out.

Unexpected betrayal tosses a young wife behind a wall of defensiveness in our next story. Can she overcome the hopelessness mashing down her very soul?

· · · • • · • • · ·

Lydia didn't notice the note until she pushed aside some of her lacy nightgowns in the drawer. Someone had wrapped ivory paper onto itself like a secret note passed in fifth grade, except this note slipped from the silky lingerie like a special chocolate kiss.

She pinched it between two fingers and lifted. Maybe a love note from Nicholas?

Music filled the bedroom, reaching an impressive crescendo. How appropriate.

"Hey, Siri, less volume."

Lydia was ready to unfold the tight square of paper. Nicholas could be so romantic. But their son interrupted.

"Mom? I'm ready to go." Tyler leaned on the doorjamb of the bedroom, his hair still damp from a fast morning shower.

"Are you taking the Rav? What time do you think you'll be home?"

Tyler looked up at the ceiling. Calculating his day. "The soccer games start at nine. I think I'm reffing most of them. So I'll probably be gone till two or three."

Their son looked tall and so grown up in his black and white referee shirt. "Don't let those kids knock you down." Lydia winked at him. What a great kid.

"They have respect for seniors." Tyler swiveled his duffel bag into the hallway, ready to leave. "See ya later. I think I'm going to the movies tonight. You and Dad can have an evening alone." He grinned and then spun to leave.

"Bye." Lydia turned back to her dresser to straighten the drawer. Morning sun painted the room in yellows and warm oranges. She had finally gotten it decorated with her favorite paintings and decorations. The house was coming together nicely. Like her life.

A quiet evening at home with Nicholas sounded nice. Romantic. She loved his sparkling blue eyes. He shared dark hair with Tyler. Lydia thought of his jokes and laughter. His helpfulness.

He'd supported her music. Her mission projects. Her teaching. He had taught Tyler to ride a bike. Later, a motorcycle. He showed Tyler his special fishing spots and never missed one of Tyler's games.

A perfect husband and father. God had blessed her.

Yes, an evening at home sounded nice.

Oh, yeah, the note.

She slowly unfolded it, savoring the quality of the paper. How long had it been there? She would owe Nicholas an apology for being oblivious. Had it been there since Valentine's Day? And this was May. Ugh.

She read: *Think you have the perfect life? Ha ha. I'm sleeping with your husband.*

Lydia dropped the paper like a hot plate, and it fluttered to the floor like a dying bird. She stepped back, bumping into the bed and stumbling backward, crashing onto the mattress. Seriously? Even the gentle music faded behind the pounding in her ears.

Nicholas stepped into their bedroom, his broad shoulders filling the doorway. "Hey, Babe, I'm going

to grab some parts to help with the church project."
He stopped, looking at her sprawled on the bed.
"What are you doing?"

She sat up. Stood up. No words came yet.

"You OK? I'm going to help put in that ramp with some other church guys. You remember, right? "

Lydia put her hand up like a police officer at an accident scene. "Stop."

"You're not sick, are you?" He started toward her.

Lydia leaned down to snatch the note. Her wrist snapped like a racquetball backhand as she thrust it toward him. "This. Read it."

He frowned as he skimmed the note. She studied his eyes, which widened. Surprised? Convicted?

"But this is a lie. This is ridiculous." He held it out. Then stopped, crumpled the note and shoved it into his jean pocket.

"Then why would some woman leave this in our bedroom? In my lingerie drawer, for Pete's sake. That's ridiculous, I agree."

"You know I'd never do something like that."

"Explain this note then."

As Lydia watched as Nicholas shifted weight. Gathered a short breath. Covered his mouth with one hand while his eyesight darted to the ceiling and then to the carpet. Then the bedspread.

And she knew.

Tears blurred the bed, the wall hangings, the carefully selected colors. Was this bedroom a metaphor for her life? A facade that hid the rot beneath. All meaningless?

Nicholas twisted the jacket with his hand. "OK. I'm sorry. I'm so sorry. Yeah, there was this one time."

"In our bedroom? In our bed?"

"I'm sorry. It'll never happen again. I'm sorry." He couldn't meet her eyes. He seemed to shrink in front of her, his shoulders folding in on himself. "It was stupid of me."

"How much time do you have before you have to leave?"

"Uh..." Nicholas looked at his watch. "Twenty minutes or so. I don't need to go. We can talk."

"We'll talk for twenty minutes. Downstairs now." She tipped her head toward the stairs outside their bedroom. He scurried away, like a puppy caught beside the mess on the floor.

He stopped off in the kitchen for a long drink of water and puttered around. Lydia could hear glasses clinking. Was he loading the dishwasher? Avoiding her?

Lydia parked herself on the leather love seat. What a joke. A love seat. He wasn't coming anywhere near it.

"I need to hear it all," she said when he tiptoed into the living room. Walking on raw eggs. They sat across the room from each other, the mahogany coffee table dividing them. She had loved the patina of this table, but it had to go. That woman had surely touched it, too.

She stared. The first person to speak lost the debate, but that person wouldn't be her. She waited.

Nicholas lost. He sighed and crossed his arms. Leaned back. "Well, I made a mistake. But it was just the one."

"One time?"

"One woman," he said. "But I love you, Lydia. Please. I don't want to get a divorce."

Lydia hugged a pillow and nestled into the soft cushion of the sofa. Further away from him. "This sofa has to go. Love seat, too." She pressed a fist into the pillow. "I'm numb, Nicholas. I haven't decided on things yet. But this is your time to come clean. First you said 'one time,' now you say 'one woman.' Which means more than one time. No more lies. Get it out, even if it's ugly."

He stared at the floor. Lydia remembered how long it had taken to find the right color for the carpet. A thick plush that caressed her toes in the evenings. They had chosen all this together. They made a good team, building a family together. A home together. And this woman had walked on her perfect carpet. And messed with her perfect husband.

"I don't want to lose our marriage. Or Tyler." He pushed out a short breath. "OK, honest time. There were three over the years."

"Three."

"I'm sorry."

"Three different women? And you brought them into our house when I was gone?"

"Yeah." Then he got up to build a fire, poking among the dead ashes. "I don't want to lose what we have."

"Quit that. It's May. We don't need a fire." Lydia needed to get away from him so she could breathe. She wandered to the dining room table. Ready to run? Ready to ask him to leave? "I don't know how we go on."

"I understand. Could we talk to Pastor Johnson? Get some counseling?"

"I don't know yet." She waved her hand at him, dismissing him. "Go. Go to the church project. They'll need you."

Nicholas stepped like a barefoot kid on a hot sidewalk. "Yeah. OK. We can talk later. I'm so sorry." Then he was gone.

Lydia pulled out her phone and called her best friend. "Jessica, can you come over this morning?"

"Uh, sure. Yes. The kids just left with Mark, so I have a few hours. Now?"

"Hurry."

By the time Jessica arrived, Lydia had brewed some coffee. She thrust a steaming mug at Jessica and plopped down at the kitchen table, her own mug on the mat in front of her.

"What's up?" Jessica sat down across from her in a vintage wooden chair. "I thought you wanted help with a project in the shop. But apparently not."

"I need to talk to someone." Lydia let the morning's events tumble out in a rush. The words burned, and she wanted them out.

Jessica drew in a breath. "Wow. Nicholas? He's Mr. Perfect. Everyone envies you."

"Not anymore."

"No." Jessica sipped her coffee. "Whew. Hot!" She put down the mug. "Are you going to forgive him?"

"I don't know. I don't even know if I got the full story. Like, when did this happen anyway?"

"Probably on one of your visits to your mother. San Diego is a long ways away."

"I suppose I have to forgive him." Lydia swirled the hot brew in her mug. Too hot to drink.

"Of course. Jesus forgave us and we need to forgive one another."

"That's easy for Jesus to say. Jesus never had his spouse commit adultery and lie about it."

Jessica sighed. "You know that's not fair."

"I know. I am just not ready yet. I thought God had blessed me with my family but, I don't know, I don't feel so blessed right now." She looked past Jessica toward the stairs. "They did it in our bed. I can't even think about that. Ugh."

"Did you talk it out this morning?"

"Hardly. I don't even know what I feel. I don't know if I want more details. Do I divorce him or is murder better?"

Jessica sighed. "I'm shocked, too. Nicholas always seemed just right for you. But God's in control."

"Maybe so, but I wish God had stopped him."

"Well–"

"What about our business?" Lydia re-focused her eyes on Jessica. "How am I going to work in the same shop with him? I don't even want to talk to him. I think I'm leaning toward murder."

Jessica ignored the felonious comment. "Are you going to get counseling?"

"I suppose. That's what you do, right? I suppose we will. He doesn't want to get a divorce. He says he's done with all the women. I just don't know what I feel. Maybe ashamed." Lydia lifted her mug, but the coffee was still too hot. She put the mug on the table and began twiddling with a napkin, twisting the blue cloth between her fingers.

"Don't feel ashamed. You did nothing wrong."

"But what if I wasn't enough?"

"Just put that aside. It's not about whether you were enough. This is all on him. He broke promises and lied."

"You sound like you know something about this."

"My dad had an affair when I was a girl. I knew about it, but my parents didn't think I did. They tried to hide it."

"I thought they were still together."

"They are. But they had a lot of hard work to do. I was so angry with my dad. Be careful how you tell Tyler."

"Maybe I won't tell Tyler. I might tell no one. Maybe I'll just—Well, I don't know what to do. We've done some pretty amazing things together, Nic and I. It's all going up in smoke. I just—I just can't see any future."

"Oh, this isn't easy. I imagine it hurts."

"Yep. I thought I had a game plan if anything like this ever happened, but I guess I'm not following the game plan. This all feels so hopeless. Like there's no good path ahead."

The next day was Sunday, and the family went to church. Like usual. Nicholas scurried around, greeting people and helping them find seats. Like usual.

She remained cemented in a seat, not even joining the worship time. Not so usual. She didn't want to sing to God today. Not feeling it. She parked in a cushioned seat in the middle of a row of cushioned seats and smiled at anyone who greeted her. It was a fake smile, but no one seemed to notice.

··•••••··

On Monday, Lydia did the morning drill. Scrambled eggs for Tyler and sent him off to school. Brewed coffee and ate some crispy toast with butter.

Nicholas had slept in the guest room and she hadn't seen him. She wasn't fixing him breakfast when she did.

Then she drove to the boutique that she and Nicholas operated. His pickup wasn't at the house, so he might be working in the back room of the shop. She unlocked the door and let the morning sun flood the store.

The warm light spilled over all the antiques, many of which they had repaired and refinished themselves. She began straightening some of the inventory. She dusted some dented galvanized buckets and rearranged a display of fragile flowered cups and saucers.

"I talked to Pastor Johnson." Nicholas stood in the doorway to the workshop. "I told him everything. He says there's hope for us."

"Good for him." Lydia didn't meet his gaze.

"I am broken. I've been pretending for a long time but I want to get right. I'm going to a men's Bible study at church this evening."

"Good for you. All that doesn't change the three women. The lies."

"If our marriage has a future, I need to change. This isn't your fault. It's mine. I want God to change me."

"Are you doing this so I don't file for divorce?" She glared at him. There were dark circles under his eyes and his hair stuck out in back. "Did you sleep at all?"

"Not really. God really hammered on me."

That was good. She turned back to her inventory dusting.

Nicholas didn't return to the shop. "Actually, I going to work on me. I hope it saves our marriage. I messed up big time. But I am making changes even if you decide to leave. Bible study is tonight. Pastor Johnson has suggested some mentors. Some accountability partners. I'm going to do what it takes."

"How will we work together? What will happen to this shop? We worked so hard on this and now—I don't know what I think."

Nicholas stepped toward her, but stopped. He held a rag drenched in smelly varnish, but he swung it behind his back. "What I did was wrong. I hurt you and I hurt us. Please don't shut out God because of me. There's still hope."

"Did you know–" It surprised Lydia how her voice trembled. "Do you know that one in three couples will experience an affair? One in three. This hurts. I didn't want to be a statistic. And I don't know why God didn't stop this."

"You wanted God to stop me?"

Lydia shrugged. "I don't know what I think. God and I aren't cool right now."

"Well, God can handle this whether you think you can or not." He straightened his shoulders. " I wasn't cool with God before, either, but that was my fault. God has been there for me this whole time, even when I was messing up. I'm starting to see that."

He ducked his head and turned back to the workshop. He stopped long enough to say, "I'm working on that chair you found on the yard sale."

"Throw that away. It's so rickety. Nobody could sit on it. I made a mistake."

"Wait till you see." He closed the workshop door behind him. Lydia straightened a silk arrangement of purple tulips.

She moved on to a display of hand-painted antique signs.

Welcome.

Blessed.

As for me and my house, we will serve the Lord.

Had she found those at a garage sale? Did Nic rehab them? Did he even think about what those signs said? What a joke of a marriage they had.

Should she try to keep the store? If they split up, who got the shop? Or the house? Or Tyler? She couldn't face that thought.

Lydia pulled out her phone and texted Jessica. "He's cooler with God than I am. Where's the justice in that?"

Jessica: *Do you think he's being genuine"*

Lydia: *Yeah, I do.*

Jessica: *What do you think your future looks like?*

Lydia: *Stinking. Maybe I want a future with Nicholas and Tyler. And even God. Not so sure about God yet, but it's not like I can quit knowing he's real.*

Jessica: *Your future looks pretty awful?*

Lydia: *Tired of looking strong. I'm a pretender. I fake it every day. At church, people assume I'm close to God. I'm a sham.*

Jessica: *Don't put up a wall. Let somebody in.*

A few customers drifted into the shop. Lydia sold the mango chalk-painted china cabinet they'd refinished together. The plates with blue flowers sold. Nicholas had found them in a box, muddy and stained. He'd cleaned them up.

He did a lot in the shop. Apparently plenty outside the shop, too. Three women. What an idiot she was.

··········

Weeks rolled by.

Nicholas was at Bible studies two nights a week and spent time on the phone with mentors. He never asked to return to their bedroom, but Lydia would often find a flower on the breakfast bar in the morning.

Could there be a future?

"I want to show you something at the shop today." Nicholas wandered through the kitchen one morning, wearing jeans and a blue t-shirt with "Live4Him" printed on the front. "Want to ride with me?"

"Not yet."

"Ok. See you there."

Lydia drank her coffee. Toasted another bagel. Searched the fridge for jelly. Wiped the countertop and scrubbed the sink. Stalled.

But she finally pushed her way into their shop. Nicholas stepped out of his workroom, wiping his hands on a red rag. He did look good in a t-shirt and jeans. Even now.

"Remember the chair?" he said.

"The ugly one? Just so you know, I didn't buy it. The sellers at that auction added it to my pile." She recalled how a chair leg looked like her broken arm from second grade. The back was broken. An arm wobbled when she grabbed it. Dry wood showed through the chipped paint. She wouldn't sit in that chair and had set it beside the dumpster.

Nic had begged her to let him try to fix it. What could he have done with that sorry chair?

"Let me show you." He extended his arm, inviting her through the door into the workshop.

Mostly curious, Lydia stepped through. She seldom came into his workshop now and it surprised her to see the projects he was working on.

Behind the workbench were his tools neatly hanging on pegboard hooks. Hammers, chisels, planes.

Dressers, desks, night stands in various stages of refurbishing piled neatly on the floor. The smell of paint and varnish filled the room. "So, where's the ugly chair?"

He pulled a tarp to reveal a chair. "I mended it. Help me decide if we ought to finish with chalk paint or maybe stain and add polyurethane."

Lydia stared. "Did you swap chairs?"

He laughed. "This is the ugly chair. Honest. Sit down." He had replaced the rails in the back of the chair, mended the legs, reinforced the seat.

"I don't think so."

"OK." He dropped onto the chair and bounced on the seat. "Solid as a rock."

"You fixed it."

Nicholas nodded and stood. "I'm learning how to fix things." He paused. His eyes searched her face and Lydia knew he was changing topics. "I need to ask. How are you doing?"

Lydia's chin trembled. Did she really want to say this? "After every church service, I cry. Every week. I hide in the back room so I can cry."

Nicholas leaned toward her. Offered his hand. She hesitated and then touched the tips of his fingers. Warm and familiar. "It's like brick by brick by brick, my wall is coming down. I built it so high I could no longer see. Who'd figure that tears could help a wall? The tears are melting the bricks. I am starting to see God's eyes again."

"I'm glad for you."

"Yeah." Why was she being this open with him? She had built a wall against him for months. Did she want him to see what was behind her wall?

Apparently she did, because the words kept tumbling out. "It's like I can reach out and embrace God. And more than that, Nic. He's drawing me into his arms. I feel his warm embrace. I am learning to relax in his arms. No more facade. It's getting comfortable. I know I belong with him."

Nicholas stepped toward her. "I love you. I don't deserve you, but I love you."

She leaned toward him. "I didn't think I had a future with God. Or with you and our marriage." She glanced past him. At his workshop and all his projects. All the items he was repairing. "I think I'm going to sit in your chair."

··········

Digging Deeper

For a time, Lydia walled off her emotions and kept God distant to her. She described the image of a brick wall. If you have ever had an experience like that, what was your wall like?

Lydia described a figurative hug into the arms of God. Have you ever experienced that? If so, how did it change you?

Lydia had a choice: to descend into hopelessness or to march forward into a future that included God's presence. How does this help you understand hope for the future?

Behind the Scenes
This story is a composite of people and stories, blended to give us a glimpse of the challenges of infidelity in a marriage, particularly how the deception can impact relationships - not just with a spouse but also with God.

Leslie's Story

Christianity doesn't deny the reality of suffering and evil ... Our hope ... is not based on the idea that we are going to be free of pain and suffering. Rather, it is based on the conviction that we will triumph over suffering.
—Brennan Manning

Even though I walk through the darkest valley, I will fear no evil, for you are with me; your rod and your staff, they comfort me.
—Psalm 23:4

•••••••••••

The heartbreak of infidelity threatened Lydia's faith walk, but God did not abandon her or her marriage. He gave her a glimpse of a better future and he welcomed her into it with open arms.

For others, the future can seem reduced to crumbles by something that was no one's fault. An accident threatens Leslie's dreams. Will she persevere when hit with indescribable hardship?

··········

A red and orange kaleidoscope of fall leaves on nearby trees glowed in the afternoon warmth. Leslie nestled into blankets on the deck of her sailboat, relishing the rock of hope realized.

Except for the pain in her neck.

Her daily adversary.

Life once had been like her sailboat, gently rocking on the waters. But that was before.

Snow had drifted through the silvery sky on that January afternoon many years before. Music from her radio filled the car with a calming melody and Leslie sang along. The fluffy new snow hid some of the gray dreariness of this winter's day in Maryland. No hint of what was coming.

The beat of the music inspired visions of choreography as she tapped her foot against the floor of the car. This song might not work for the ballroom dances but maybe for swing?

Traffic was normal. Plenty of vehicles, but nothing unusual. Good. She wouldn't be late for her appointment. Her right shoulder ached slightly, but each of these physical therapy appointments helped her to deal with that dance injury. Her physical therapist, Sam, had been amazing so far with her rehab.

She drew the car to a stop behind a tractor trailer, waiting for the red light to change to green. No need to fret over a traffic light. She wasn't late. All was fine.

A few more rehab sessions and she'd be back at her workout routine, lifting weights, dancing aerobics, and bicycling.

She loved her life. At 39, she was still single, but God might gift her with a husband and children yet. No rush. Contentment settled on Leslie like the feathery flakes drifting to the road.

And then a truck slammed into the back of Leslie's car, whipping her body forward and backward several times, like a rag doll in the teeth of the family dog. The groan of crumpled metal faded quickly, but glass tinkled as it dropped to the asphalt.

Leslie drew in a deep breath. Unbuckled her seatbelt. Slipped out of her car. "Thanks, Lord," she whispered as she turned toward the large delivery truck pressed against her car's trunk.

The young driver raced up to her, eyes wide like a kid caught peeling the wrapper off of a lollipop that his mom had said he couldn't have.

"I'm all right." Leslie had already done a quick pat down of herself. No blood or broken bones. "Let's exchange information. It's fine."

They exchanged names and phone numbers. Then Leslie continued to her appointment, where Sam checked her over and sent her home.

Her car was more battered than Leslie was, but they could both putter home. By the time she walked through the front door of her apartment, the snowfall had thickened. Soon, the roads were impassable.

She phoned her doctor from her living room sofa.

"With this snowstorm, it will be safer for you to stay home and rest. I don't think you need to come in," the doctor said. "You'll probably feel sore tomorrow, but you'll be okay."

Leslie had experienced tender muscles after some early dance classes and long bike rides. But her next-morning soreness was unexpected.

She ached like someone had taken batting practice on her body. Her head felt heavy. Bowling-ball kind of heavy. How was her strained neck supporting it?

She tenderly touched her bruised ribs. Pain radiated from her lower back and left leg. She could only raise her right arm a few inches.

She called her doctor, who quickly referred her to Sam for more physical therapy.

"Let's see what happened now." Sam had Leslie sit on his examining table and ran his hands along her spine. "Got your dance classes rescheduled yet?"

"Soon. First, you need to do your work. I hope this car accident doesn't slow us down too much."

Sam chuckled. "Yes." And then he stopped. "I need to talk to your doctor." He left her sitting alone in the cool room as he hot-stepped it into his office.

Leslie might have shifted to a padded chair, but the thought of moving made her teeth clench together. She'd just hold still until he got back.

While she waited, Leslie reviewed her dance steps in her mind. She didn't want to forget some of the complex moves once her body was back in shape. Some say it's like riding a bike: muscle memory never loses the technique. Leslie wasn't sure if that was true. Better to practice, even in her imagination for now.

She could find out soon.

Sam's return wasn't swift, but when he walked back into the room, he held an open book. "Leslie, it appears you have major nerve damage to your back and shoulder." He pointed to a page with full-color illustrations of the nerves weaving through the body like the city's highway system.

"It will get better, right?" The drawing made little sense, and Leslie was eager to return to her job. She loved interpreting sign language for the deaf. That was as fulfilling as her dance classes. Maybe more.

This annoying shoulder injury had already kept her out of work and slowed her dancing. She wanted to get back to her life.

Sam hesitated. Leslie couldn't read his face. "I don't know," he said. "I've only seen this kind of injury in textbooks."

So that's what he held. A textbook.

Then he explained. Because of the prior injury, Leslie's shoulder had not held up under the impact of the crash. "You have a winging right scapula. Your long thoracic nerve is severed."

She cocked her head to one side. "Amateur language?"

He blew a quick breath. "Your shoulder blade sticks out from your back because the serrates anterior muscle is barely functioning."

Leslie blinked. "You'll need to show me the pictures. What is the serrates anterior muscle?"

"One of the largest muscles in the human body." He pointed to a broad muscle under the armpit. "You need to consult a specialist." He closed the book with a slap.

"So give me a list of specialists. I want this fixed. You've been great, Sam, and I need your suggestions."

Leslie left her appointment that day with a long list of specialists.

Over the next few months, time slowed. Physical therapy and doctor appointments were mixed together like a partially frozen river with slush, ice, and water flowing downstream.

Each doctor heard the same description: "My whole body is screaming at me with pain."

Each doctor replied, "Give it time."

None of the specialists were confident of a solution beyond physical therapy and time.

Over the next two years, "giving it time" cost Leslie her career, her dancing, her exercise routine, and many of her friends. Activities and appointments often had to be canceled at the last minute because of unrelenting soreness.

Her roommate, Zoe, stayed.

Zoe had curly dark hair, and a bright smile that seldom dimmed. The two talked over coffee one morning, sitting at their small wooden kitchen table, yellow sunlight streaming through the window. "How are things going?"

"Not great," Leslie said. "I feel like I'm not a great friend anymore. Not since the accident. "

"Yeah, well, you hurt. I totally get it." Zoe sipped from a big blue mug emblazoned *Faith and Future*. That was a Zoe kind of motto.

"It's agony." Leslie hadn't described how the pain could roll in like the tide, a dull constant ache. Or like waves slammed by a storm, deep and intense. Sometimes the pain was like a Category 4 hurricane, seizing her body and pulsing with muscle spasms that erupted into nausea.

"How are you sleeping?"

"Not well." Even when sleeping in a nest of four pillows, some nights Leslie saw each hour tick by.

"Are you doing okay with your finances?"

"I have some savings," Leslie said. "And a tiny disability check. It isn't much. My cousin said I could answer the phone at his business when I was able. But not much income. I'm sorry, Zoe. I'm not sure I can hold up my end of things in our apartment."

"Of course you can stay," Zoe touched the back of her hand. "You can't afford to live alone, anyway. We can share costs this way."

"I want to pay what I can."

Zoe ignored that offer. "The next thing we need to tackle is this depression." She sipped her coffee. With that mug. Zoe mugs could almost out-blast her smile. Way too cheery for this discussion. Faith and Future? Death and heaven looked better than this.

The familiar blackness pressed on her again. She'd tried to push it back before, but it was too heavy to lift. And Zoe wanted to tackle it?

Leslie coveted a little self-pity. It seemed more comfortable than sitting in a bright kitchen with a cheery roommate who didn't realize how awful this was. "I can't see anything in the future, Zoe. I can barely see God."

Zoe glanced at her watch. "Ugh! I am going to be late for work. I hope there's no traffic. But I'm not leaving you without some homework."

"Homework? I suppose I should practice my Zoe smiles all day?"

Zoe laughed. "No, but God has things to say to us when we're down. I'm giving you a verse to think about today while I'm gone."

Leslie felt her eyes roll. She hoped Zoe hadn't seen that. "Homework, huh?"

"You can do this. Here's your verse. Read it. Memorize it. Read it again. Think about what God is saying to you."

"My brain isn't awake enough for that."

Zoe laughed. "No, probably not. But do it anyway." She pulled an index card from her leather Bible and jotted something. "Let this verse be a light for your day. Okay, I need to go. I want to hear what God says to you."

Light for the day? What did Zoe know about this darkness? God was on the other side of dull days, dominated by chronic pain. Zoe didn't understand this pain. Did God?

But Leslie reached for her Bible and a notebook. Zoe would ask later what she'd done, so Leslie needed to do something. She found the verse and copied it into her notebook.

"Jeremiah 29:11. 'For I know the plans I have for you,' says the Lord. 'They are plans for good and not for disaster, to give you a future and a hope.'"

Leslie dropped her pen on the table. She couldn't do this.

Instead, she limped back to her bedroom, lowered herself into the bed, and covered her head with blankets. Her nest of pillows cradled her.

She must have slept because the key in the front door startled her. Zoe was home already?

Leslie gently forced her legs over the edge of the bed and pushed herself up. Slowly. She ought to speak to Zoe, so she shuffled into the kitchen. Her back and shoulders screamed at her and Leslie almost turned back. But Zoe saw her.

"Hi, Leslie!" Zoe carried two bags of groceries. Stalks of celery poked out of one of the sacks. She shined a Zoe smile at Leslie. "I've been looking forward to your report all day. What did you learn from the verse I gave you?"

Leslie didn't answer.

Zoe sorted fresh veggies in piles beside the sink. "I'm making stir-fry tonight." She stopped for a moment to study Leslie. "You worked on it, didn't you?"

"Yes." Leslie put a hand on the kitchen table to support her as she lowered herself into the chair. "Well, no, not really."

"Okay. Well, want to talk about it?"

"I thought a lot about the accident. I asked God questions. Such as, why didn't he protect me?" Leslie felt a knot forming in her throat and she stopped. Tears blossomed in her eyes.

"What did God say to you?"

Leslie swallowed hard, trying to dissolve the knot. "I remembered something. At the moment of the accident, I saw a tractor trailer in front of me. I only had time to yell 'Jesus!' That was my prayer. The light changed." Leslie paused, drumming her fingers on the table where she sat. "The light changed, Zoe. The tractor trailer pulled away just as I was being pushed into him. Or most likely under him."

Zoe's knife sliced through vegetables in a rhythmic chunk-chunk-chunk. "What do you think would have happened if he hadn't moved?"

"I wouldn't be talking with you right now."

"So God was there."

"I'm tired of hurting," Leslie said. She would have banged her fist on the table just to show her frustration, but she knew better. "I'm tired of all these medicines." She waved her hand at the prescription bottles in the middle of the table. "I'm tired of physical therapy. Tomorrow I have another appointment. I'm tired of it."

"Understandable. Just don't get bitter. You've never been bitter. Now's not the time to start."

"Is the stir-fry done yet? I'm not sure if I ate today."

"Trying to distract me?" Zoe flashed those white teeth again. "It is nearly done." She pulled two blue plates off an open shelf.

"You have your book club tonight, right?"

"I do, but I can stay if you need to talk."

"Let's eat, then you go. I just need to think, I guess." Or not think. Or blame God some more. Or review all the pain and how she didn't deserve it. It could be a good evening of hot pity.

"Here you go." Zoe laid a filled plate before Leslie and then swung a little white vase onto the center of the table. She pushed a single yellow daisy into the vase. "Maybe this will brighten your evening."

Zoe sat down, and they prayed over their meal. Then she lifted her eyebrows in a Harrison Ford sad-puppy look as she watched Leslie. "I'm so sorry. You know God didn't cause your accident, right?"

"I know," Leslie said.

"And I believe he can use it for good in your life."

"I can't see that yet. But I'll try. That's the least I can do since you made my favorite stir-fry."

"So I had a little boy today who came into the classroom after lunch. Sobbing. Big tears and red face. I went rushing over and got him calmed down. 'What's wrong?' I asked him. He said, 'Annie was singing the Gummy Bear song in line and I don't like the Gummy Bear song!' Phew, kindergarteners."

Zoe usually told funny stories at dinner, and Leslie usually laughed along with her. But not tonight. She ate in silence.

When Zoe finally escorted her bright smile out the door for her book club meeting, Leslie stared at the tiny kitchen.

The sink had a single bowl, and the workspace on each side was less than three feet. A narrow stove and small refrigerator with rounded corners filled the end of the room. An old tiny kitchen in a fading tiny apartment.

And this was now all Leslie could afford. Not even this much if Zoe wasn't carrying most of the weight.

What kind of future did she have? Peering into her future was like trying to see in a black cave. Or maybe in a dark train tunnel with a locomotive churning toward her. She could hear it coming, but no idea when it'd emerge.

God, how could you let this happen to me? I want to dance again. I miss bike rides in the park. This pain is too much for me. When will it end?

Leslie pushed herself up from the table and carried her plate to the sink. She needed a shower before therapy tomorrow. Did she try that this evening? Decisions that once seemed so simple now stumped her.

The shower would hurt. The therapy would hurt. It helped, but it hurt.

Leslie shuffled back to the living room and stopped. "God, I can't do this. Not today." She sank to the couch but barely caught the edge and continuing sinking to the floor. How much lower could she go?

She sat on the tan carpet and felt its soft surface against her outstretched legs. She couldn't even sit down correctly anymore.

Tears began to flow. The room blurred behind tears as though she were seeing the chair and lamp through smeared glass.

Darkness loomed above her like black water closing over her head. She felt imaginary chains around her ankles, dragging her deeper into the gloom.

She sprawled onto her stomach, letting the cool carpet cushion her body. "It isn't fair, God. This isn't what I planned. This isn't the life I want."

Hot words tumbled out as she sobbed. Snot ran down her face and she pounded her fists into the carpet. "It's not fair, God. Not right. Where are you?"

Pounding her fists made her whole upper body hurt. She can't even have a meltdown without inflicting more pain. This is her life now? She couldn't go on. It was too much. She sobbed and sobbed.

She couldn't see the light above her anymore, as the dark water seemed to close around her. She was alone in this darkness. Sinking fast. No one around. No one to hear her as she dropped. Could she go on alone in this darkness of depression and despair?

It was too much to bear. She had to do something.

She thrust an arm up toward where she had imagined the glow had been, through the murky waters of her mind, reaching for a hint of light. Reaching for the Comforter.

"God..." she choked out words. "If it's like this for the rest of my life... if all I can do for the rest of my life is sit in my recliner... I'll do it... but please, please never leave me, Jesus. Please don't leave me!"

Leslie blinked. Trying to see beyond the vaseline glass. Trying to see beyond the black waters trying to swallow her.

And she did.

She was certain that Jesus was sitting on the floor beside her, stroking her tangled hair. His gentle hand started at her crown and followed her hair to her back. Then he repeated the motion. Gentle hands. Over and over, he stroked her head. Softly. Lovingly.

He was with her.

The chains around her ankles started snapping. Links popped, and then she could feel herself rising. Freed from the darkness. Almost like she could fly.

Her imagination still worked.

Tears evaporated, and her heartbeat slowed to normal. She remained on the floor for a time, letting Jesus' presence comfort her. Imagining his hand on her head.

Then Leslie slowly pushed herself up onto the couch and shuffled to the kitchen table where she had left her Bible.

"Lord, let's try this again. *Jeremiah 29:11. You have plans for me.*" She began to write.

She had a story to tell Zoe.

・・・●・●・●・・

Years later, Leslie would recall that image of Jesus with her. "My pain is no longer as severe, but I don't want to forget that moment. He was the hope in the middle of the worst day ever."

Digging Deeper

Most of us have not endured pain like Leslie's pain. But how does her experience help you in your own hardship - or perhaps in another's difficulties?

Leslie found she never wanted to lose God in her life. What are ways she sought God's presence?

Behind the Scenes

I met Leslie several years ago at a writers' conference and did not know the pain she was in. She exuded kindness, intelligence, and faithfulness. Her story is true. I added some fictional elements to the story, such as naming the physical therapist and combining different women into Zoe's character.

Zoe's Help

Loss pushes us to difficult places where we have not been before. We often question whether or not we have the courage and stamina to survive the pain. However, we often are given gifts that tell us that we are not alone and that we can withstand the journey.
—Susan Barbara Apollon

May the God of hope fill you with all joy and peace as you trust in him, so that you may overflow with hope by the power of the Holy Spirit.
—Romans 15:13

· · · • • · • • · · ·

Leslie found hope in spite of her circumstances. Her pain didn't keep her from some amazing life developments. It might have actually helped her. How does she navigates new opportunities? Is she also able to direct Zoe through a challenging situation?

· · · • • · • • · · ·

Days and weeks rolled into months and months of gray throbbing pain for Leslie after the car accident. She might have inched into the life of a hermit, but Zoe was having none of it.

"Did you hear about the singles group at church?" Zoe sat in a well-worn chair in their postage-stamp living room. She glanced up from the book she was reading, *The Pursuit of God* by Tozer. "You should go."

"What made you think of that?"

"I'm using the church bulletin as a bookmark and saw the blurb." Zoe's smile was bigger than usual. "I thought of you."

"You're single, too."

"I'm dating. And he could be the one. I'm not shopping right now."

Leslie had nestled into a thick cocoon of pillows and blankets on the couch. And had the almost-always-present ice pack around her neck. "But I couldn't go to that group."

"And why not?"

Leslie swept her hand over her shoulder, body and pillows the same way Vanna White showed a winning phrase on *Wheel of Fortune*. "Because I can't take all this with me and I never know when I'll need them."

"But sometimes you go out. And I think you'd meet some new friends. Why don't you plan to go? If the pain gets too overwhelming, then you could stay home. Or leave early if you have to." Zoe still held her book open. Obviously, she expected to win quickly and return to her reading.

Leslie twisted her mouth in thought. Zoe had Paul. They'd probably marry some day and Leslie wanted a relationship like that. "But who would be interested in a relationship with me? I can't commit to anything. You know how it is. The pain flares up when I don't expect it."

Zoe waved a hand. "There's another meeting next week. Just pray about it."

"I used to think about marriage, you know. But who would marry a woman with chronic pain? No career. No income. That's not in my future anymore. I'm not a fun date." She twisted her mouth to the side. "There's no future with me."

"But maybe you'd make new friends."

"True." Leslie blew air through pursed lips. "So many friends peeled off when I couldn't do the things we did together. I still miss dancing. And I'd love a nice Saturday afternoon hike." She sighed. "I think the pain was hard for some of them to understand. New friends would be nice."

"Pain shouldn't control your life."

Leslie didn't answer. Why shouldn't it? Pain had stolen her hobbies, her career, most of her friends. Why not steal her life, too?

"That's easy for someone not in pain to say." There. Zoe needed to know what was true. Leslie raised her eyes to see if her words doused Zoe's big smile.

They didn't. Zoe's teeth sparkled. "I trust your faith and in God's strength. Let's see what he stirs in you."

Sometimes Zoe could be so annoyingly correct.

Well, maybe just this once Leslie could try.

So she attended the meeting, expecting nothing. She ventured gingerly into the host's living room and scanned the crowd. Nobody she knew. Why was this a good idea again?

She wandered into the kitchen, where plates of assorted snacks hid the countertops. Chips and dip. Sliders. A fruit plate with strawberries, blueberries, and raspberries. Another plate of cauliflower and celery sticks. Health food corner. Oh, there were the chips and cookies.

"New here?"

Leslie looked up to see a tall man with salt and pepper hair balancing a plate of snacks. "First time for me."

"Me, too. I'm Richard."

"Leslie."

They shook hands, and he leaned back against the cabinet. "So tell me something about yourself."

Leslie laughed. "Oh, that would be a long story."

Richard shrugged, then dipped a chip into Ranch dressing. "I have time."

And so Leslie gave him the short version of the story. The accident. The appointments. Not the sobbing yet. No point in dumping the entire load. He might finish the snacks and bolt. She smiled. "And what's your story?"

"I know a little about hard times." He crunched into an Oreo. "I lost my wife to cancer two years ago. We had an amazing marriage." His voice trailed off, and he looked up at the ceiling for a moment. But then he focused on Leslie again. "I didn't come here to find a wife. I'm here with some of the guys on my volleyball team."

"Oh, I didn't come to find a relationship. Just to make new friends."

Richard passed her for an empty plate. "Grab some snacks and we'll get acquainted."

By the time the evening ended, Leslie had a date on her calendar.

At dinner the next night, Zoe dove in with questions. "So, what do you know about this man?" She ladled a stew for their dinner and set two bowls on the little kitchen table. Sitting down across from Leslie, she said a quick prayer for the meal.

"He lost his wife to cancer two years ago, but they had a wonderful life together. They both loved to sail."

"He has a sailboat?" Zoe leaned forward, the spoon in midair. "I wonder if he'd take Paul and me out? A romantic evening sailing trip would be so cool."

"I'm sure he would." Leslie filled her spoon with stew. Zoe had placed new orange flowers on the table and a pretty yellow checked tablecloth. "He's a very kind man."

Zoe dipped her spoon. "He's a believer, right?"

"Of course. He even prayed for my pain last night."

"So you told him."

"Not everything, but yes. There will be time for more later."

Zoe nodded. "Aren't you glad I talked you into going?" She twisted her mouth to the side like she did when she had more to say. She didn't say it yet.

Leslie laughed and threw her head back, letting a mild pain jolt her shoulder. It was worth it. "Right. You get all the credit."

"Now we're in a race now to see who gets engaged first." Zoe's eyes sparkled.

"I don't know about that."

But God was already weaving his wounded children together. Leslie and Richard continued to date.

At one point, Leslie questioned Richard: "Why would you want to be a part of my life, with this pain?"

"Pain can't control our lives." Richard smiled, his blue eyes dancing with love. "As Linda and I went through her cancer illness, I learned more than ever the importance of *who* you are with, not just *what* you do together. I think we make a good team. We'll manage."

Their wedding was on May 1, 2004, and on that day, Leslie Basil married Richard Payne.

Pain wanted to rule Leslie's life, and now she was Mrs. Payne. God had a sense of humor, too.

Marriage to Richard brought her new friends and fresh adventures.

"You'll love sailing," Richard said.

"How much pain will sailing cause?"

"We'll figure out strategies."

He found a soft beanbag to cradle Leslie's fragile body during the sailing motion. Leslie found that frequent breaks, lying down in the cockpit, rested her neck. Sometimes she strapped on a cervical collar.

And when pain flared, and her body ached, Richard pulled out the beanbag. Leslie nestled into it, her whole body supported in a cozy nest.

Richard and Leslie maintained a morning routine, even on the sailboat, where Richard prayed for those in need, asking for, "The Lord's physical touch and spiritual presence."

Every morning, Leslie jumped up and down inside. *Me, me, me! Please heal me.* Would God give her that request?

The interior of the sailboat had polished dark wood and soft cushions. In the afternoons, when they were sailing for days, Leslie would lay her leather notebook on the glossy wooden tabletop and write long sentences. Recalling her day. Her emotions. Sometimes she described a sunset on the ocean or the birds that landed on the bow.

Richard sat across from her at the table, sipping coffee. "I think you should write for other people to read."

"Oh, my, I couldn't. I haven't really written for years. Just my journals." She chuckled. "In my journal, I can rant and complain in private." She rolled her favorite pen between her thumb and fingers. A good pen and lovely paper helped her write with enthusiasm.

"You write about what God's done for you, right?"

"Of course." She reached out and grasped his muscular hand. The lines and bends were already familiar to her. She ran her finger over his strong knuckle. "And there are so many things I've written. Including our story."

"You've got a gift. I really think you should write more."

Leslie stared at him. A new pain, of others rejecting her words, flared up like a bonfire. "What if no one wants to read what I've written? What if my work gets criticized?"

He shrugged. "No pain, no gain. What was that project you've talked about?"

Ah, Smitty Smith. Leslie smiled. Smitty was her father's best friend, and she'd heard his stories many times. She could see his now-elderly face in her mind. "Smitty asked me to write his life story."

Richard nodded. "You should do that."

"I'm not sure if I can do it. It could be a lot of work. I'd need to do more research. Interviews. And write. What if this pain knocks me out of the project?" But even as she objected, a spark of excitement flickered.

"Pain had already won if you never start." Richard squeezed her hand. "Try it. You never know."

Well, she'd gone to a singles get-together in spite of her pain and noticed what God had done. Maybe pain wouldn't be the final answer.

So Leslie pursued the project. Smitty Smith was an icon in his community, honored by everyone who knew him. She spent hours with him, listening to his stories and reliving the past years.

His life was a story of pain, too. Not like her pain, but the pain that hurts the heart and emotions. During the Great Depression, Smitty was "a colored shoeshine boy" in the poorest neighborhood of Baltimore City. He thought he was a nobody. Too much of life reinforced that idea. Nobody Smith. But God had a different opinion of Smitty.

Smitty died before Leslie finished the book. She attended the huge memorial service which honored Smitty's life.

Leslie persevered with the book and finished it soon after Smitty's death. Dr. Tony Evans, Smitty's nephew, wrote the foreword for the finished book, which was published under the title of *The Legacy of Nobody Smith*.

"I knew you could do this." Richard held the book up, studying the cover. "I'm very impressed."

"Any attention this book has is probably because of Dr. Evans' foreword." Leslie picked up a second book, running her hand over the glossy cover. "But I hope any impact it has is for God's glory."

Richard nodded. "I'm sure that will be true."

"Smitty was an incredible man of God," Leslie said. "The only reason he picked me to write his story, out of all the people he knew, was because I am Irv's daughter. He loved my dad and I think he loved me, too."

"That's a good enough reason."

・・・●●●・・・

One day, between sailboat trips, Leslie and Zoe met for lunch at a small cafe, the kind with modest round tables and trendy curtains. Some customers could sit outside along the edge of the sidewalk. Leslie and Zoe sat inside.

"How's married life?" Zoe rose from her chair as Leslie approached. Hugs. Not a quick barely-know-you hug but a hug of long connection.

Leslie smiled as they settled into the white wicker chairs. "Marriage is more than I deserve. But I could ask you the same." A single flower and a teal linen tablecloth decorated their table. Maybe this was where Zoe had gotten her kitchen table inspirations when they shared an apartment.

"It's awesome! I love being married." Zoe scanned the menu and gave an order to the smiling waitress. Then she began to shuffle the slender salt shaker with her finger. Back and forth. "Paul threw me a curve this week, though."

"What's up?"

Zoe shifted in her chair. "He wants to start his own business. He's an amazing carpenter and wants to do house renovations."

"I know he's very skilled. That's exciting news." Leslie leaned forward. "Wait, you said he threw you a curve?"

"I'm afraid. We want to start a family and I'd like to quit work for a few years to spend time with our kids. But we can't lose my income if he does this."

"What does Paul say about that?" Leslie grabbed the salt shaker before Zoe wore out the tablecloth with her shuffling.

Zoe smiled, but this one was more lopsided. A little ruthful. "He says we'll be fine. We've prayed about this a lot and he wants a family. And his own business. He says he could help me more if he could set his own hours."

"He's thought about this. So why are you fearful?"

Zoe looked down at the table. Searching for the salt shaker again? Leslie held on to it. Zoe looked up, her hands waving without a shaker for stability.

"What if he doesn't earn enough to pay our bills? What if he can't find work like he thinks he can? What if we have to postpone children for a while? Forever?"

"Oh, my, this isn't like you at all. You were my rock back when we roomed together. You never let all my problems get you down."

"Well, I love you, but it's easier to be strong about somebody else's fear than when it's mine."

Leslie laughed. "That's honest."

Zoe laughed then, too. "How did you handle your fear? When it looked like nothing was going like you planned?"

"It was the grace of God. I wanted to give up. He wouldn't let me."

"How do I go on? I'm afraid we'll end up homeless and babyless."

"No, you aren't."

"No, I'm not." Zoe giggled. "Maybe blown a little out of proportion? Let's change the subject before I get rolling again. So, how are you doing?"

"The pain is always there, of course. I wanted God to heal me in those days. Still do, really. Richard prays for that every morning."

"I'm glad he does that."

"The pain is better. I can manage it more easily with medication and therapy. And my pillows." Leslie remembered the long days nestled into a pillow of blankets and soft props. "But I've told the Lord that I'm like the woman who touched the hem of his garment. You know that story?"

"Of course. She had a bleeding issue for a long time. She was out of hope." Zoe flashed her best smile when the perky waitress delivered green and orange salads and cups of chowder.

Leslie nodded. "Yes, her. I told the Lord that I'm reaching out and grabbing hold of Jesus like she did. I'm not letting go."

Zoe crunched into her salad and then pointed her fork at Leslie. "Good for you. I need to learn from your perseverance."

"It's not so romantic." Leslie savored the chowder. "Sometimes I feel like I'm dragging behind God, bumping along on the road, the dirt and sand getting in my face. It's not turning out like I want."

"I can tell you're a writer." Zoe laughed. "That's a powerful word picture."

"It could be discouraging. But I'm not discouraged anymore. God is with me and there's the hope."

"So I think you're telling me to trust God for our future, too. I guess I got a little dramatic, huh?"

"*Homeless and babyless*? Maybe a bit."

"Maybe." Zoe sipped her iced tea. "I thought my future resembled a bird. It just flew up and left me."

"I understand. What I feel is all by his grace. I can't do it alone. No way. No how. But it's like Jesus strokes my hair. He lets me sob and fight until I surrender one more time. Then he helps me wipe my nose and sets me off with a new future and hope for the moment. That holds me for quite a while. Until the next time I tell him I can't do this any longer."

"It's amazing to hear you talk about hope." Zoe turned to her soup. "Your pain... Whew, I know how it got you down. It's hard to have hope in the future when the present looks impossible. But you're doing it."

"I decided pain will not stop me. I don't want fear paralyzing me." Leslie jabbed her fork into her salad. "Oh! I wanted to tell you something else that I learned."

"Okay."

"You know how during the Covid shutdown, when we were all stuck inside and people started purging their houses since they were home, anyway?"

"I did some of that. It was amazing how much stuff we'd accumulated. Stuff we didn't need." Zoe waved her hands briefly. "So much stuff."

"Exactly. Well, I did the same thing. And I found forty years' worth of journals."

Zoe pushed her salad bowl aside and glanced at the door, where a small group laughed as they entered the cafe. "You were always journaling. I remember that. You read them, right?"

"Of course I did." Leslie smiled. "It was amazing. I read the sweeping story of my life. And I could see how God faithfully wove all the threads of my life into a beautiful story only he could write."

"I've often wondered how hindsight plays into our understanding of who God is."

Leslie nodded. "He wasted nothing. It was incredible. He used it all. Heartbreaks, illness, injuries, travel, adventures, dreams disappointments. All of it. He gave me a beautiful story."

"Amazing."

"I was on a high for days after I read my life story."

"I've always wanted to ask this, watching you work through your pain. Do you have a favorite verse to keep you going?"

Leslie gave another quick smile, confident as a small bird soaring toward the sun. "Romans 15:13. It says, *'May the God of hope fill you with all joy and peace as you trust in him, so that you may overflow with hope by the power of the Holy Spirit.'*"

Zoe lifted her mug of tea. "There's that hope again."

"Yes, hope again. I have to learn to trust God. God will not stop being who he is. Hope is not based on me or my actions. It's all him. What he's done in the past, he will do again."

"Hence your discovery from your journals," Zoe said. "You've seen what God's done in the past."

"Yes!" Leslie quickly tapped the tablecloth. "I choose to trust. My trust is in the God of hope. He is the source of hope. And you know what he gives me in exchange for my trust?"

"What?" Zoe leaned in, her eyes fixed on Leslie's face.

"I become filled with joy and peace." Leslie set aside her bowl and spoon.

"I need that tradeoff."

"You can have it, too. This is real. I am more joyful since the pain entered my life."

·········

Digging Deeper
Write out the major occurrences in your life, especially noticing the high and low points. Despite her chronic pain, Leslie can see how God has been at work in her life's story. Write ways you can see how God has been at work in your life story.

Leslie connected the future that God offers with peace. How does that idea, as expressed in Romans 15:13, encourage you?

Behind the Scenes
Although parts of this story are fictional, I have used Leslie's words to express her trust in God. She leans on Romans 15:13 as a strong corner post in her life.

Leslie's book, *The Legacy of Nobody Smith*, is still available for purchase from Amazon.

I am also grateful to Leslie for helping me with details and other writerly suggestions for her chapters. She is a special friend.

The Final Chapter

" How strange this fear of death is! We are never frightened at a sunset."
—George Macdonald

"Those who trust in the Lord will find new strength. They will soar high on wings like eagles. They will run and not grow weary. They will walk and not faint."
—Isaiah 40:31

·········

As I was putting the final touches on this book, tragedy became a muscular MMA* fighter which slammed me to the mat, put a knee on my throat, and then snarled, "So, now do you really believe all this stuff you've been writing about?" My body ached as though I was trying to climb what seemed like an oxygen-deprived, muscle-draining Colorado 14er**. My heart pounded. What happened yes-

terday was blurred. Why did I make that particular decision a month ago? No idea.

But I owed that MMA opponent an answer. Did I really believe all this stuff that I write about? Even when it happened to me? When that adversary stole my breath and my comfort? Did I really believe in hope?

Here's my story.

⋯⋯••••••⋯

"I think you need to take me to the ER." Matt leaned on our dining room table, his body doubled up, his left hand cradling his belly.

My husband had been fighting some discomfort all day, but this pain seemed to have multiplied in the last hour or so.

Did he have a kidney infection? That had been his assumption, but now, as evening was turning into night, the tenderness had intensified into hard boxing jabs to his abdomen.

So I drove him to the emergency room on that frosty January night. Once we cleared all the admissions paperwork, the medical staff drew blood, checked vitals, did a CT scan. Finally, the doctor came back in. "We think you passed a kidney stone. We're not seeing anything in the scan."

We went home, and in the morning, there was no pain. So the diagnosis seemed reasonable.

But within two weeks, Matt's primary doctor reached out to him to do another CT scan, this time one with a dye to better differentiate any issues. This second scan showed a mass in his kidney.

By mid-February, Matt faced a biopsy, although the surgeon was confident the mass was cancerous. The primary treatment for kidney cancer is the removal of the diseased kidney.

So, on March 1, Matt had a kidney removed.

"Everything looked good," the surgeon told me as Matt was in the recovery room after surgery. "I saw nothing to show that the cancer had broken through."

He was wrong. A biopsy showed that this cancer had escaped through the kidney wall.

Surely only a few cells, I reasoned. Surely a short round of treatment—maybe chemo, maybe radiation—would get this problem under control quickly and we'd get on with our lives.

Matt did well after the surgery. Every night, after he brushed his teeth, he'd pull up his t-shirt. "Belly check time." Every night, I'd study the incisions in his stomach—the five slots where a robot had sliced through his belly to free his kidney.

"Looks good." I told him that every night. The incisions healed nicely, with no infection.

He seemed to be making a quick return to life as we knew it. Matt spent a couple of weeks resting in the house, but soon could wander out to his shop to work on projects for a couple of hours every day. The tinkering sessions got longer each day.

Everything appeared to be on track.

But it wasn't.

Shortly after the follow-up meeting with the surgeon, we met with the therapy team. First, the chemo doctor gave us unexpected news. "This cancer is very aggressive. It's a bad one." But he wasn't sure if radiation or chemotherapy would happen first. They wanted to do more testing. And they had to wait for six weeks before starting any treatments so that the incisions from the kidney removal were fully healed.

Matt, being his practical self, learned of a chemo class offered by the hospital and signed us up immediately. There, we learned about life during chemotherapy.

Basically, they would try to kill him every three weeks and then let his body recuperate. The cancer cells, they told us, couldn't recover, but his healthy cells could. So the plan was to spend the summer in the tidal wave of chemotherapy, dying and recovering.

Matt found an audio book coupling cancer treatments with movement. He listened intently and began a notebook where he could log daily information, everything from his temperature and blood pressure to his pain level. And his exercise. He lifted some light weights and made sure he walked a half hour a day.

"I want you to put that picture from New Dawn on the front." He handed me his new notebook.

We were both part of a ministry, New Dawn Ministries of Hope. The organization's logo included a bright orange sun rising from the horizon. I pulled up the file for the ministry and designed a cover for his notebook that included part of the logo. "Could you add, 'Working toward a healthier tomorrow'?" he said.

Yes, I could.

"You may have to keep this notebook once we get chemo going," he warned me. I promised I would, although he was the meticulous detail person in our family. I knew this would stretch me, but I would do it.

All the chemo details soon became like a roaring behemoth to me, rising on the horizon in a snarling march toward us. This monster rose like whirling storm clouds, a strong wind blasting us with gritty, cold air.

I knew the summer would be like none I'd ever had.

·········

By late March, pain became Matt's regular companion. He avoided Percocet and other strong narcotics so he could still drive. But one evening, driving himself home, pain slammed him so hard that he sat paralyzed when a stoplight changed from red to green.

"I couldn't drive at all. I just sat there," he told me later. Finally, the pain eased enough that he could pull into a gas station at the corner and wait till the pain subsided.

One morning, at 3 am, he sat down on the edge of our bed and gently nudged me awake. "I'm having a lot of pain." He put his hand to his abdomen again. "I don't think I can take any more Ibuprofen."

His surgeon had warned him to limit his Ibuprofen use since it was hard on the remaining kidney. He had a prescription for Percocet, but Matt was nervous about its powerful side effects. Like no driving. And addiction.

So that was the issue he was tossing around in the night, while enduring excruciating pain. "I think we need some help," I told him. "Let's go to the ER."

"I can drive myself. I didn't want to bother you."

"Uh, no. No way. I am taking you. Let me get dressed."

At the hospital, Matt endured another round of blood work and another CT scan. The staff had no solutions except "take those pain meds sooner to stay on top of the pain."

That didn't help much. Pain rolled in like an English fog, thick enough to cut.

Doctors ordered another biopsy to discover if the cancer had entered lymph nodes. Once the biopsy was done, we waited and tried to settle back into some kind of normalcy.

Matt's doctors suspected he had an infection in his abdominal area causing the pain, and so began bombarding him with antibiotics. When the first antibiotic didn't seem to do much, the medical staff tried a second - to discover that he was allergic to it.

A third antibiotic did little except cause severe constipation.

The pain gained momentum, gripping him in its powerful fist.

His medical staff kept swapping antibiotics. Was the pain from the cancer? They weren't willing to say that. They were stumped. Why weren't the antibiotics working?

April 13 was a special day for Matt and me. A dear friend was getting married that evening and, months before, had asked me to photograph her wedding.

In a week of medical appointments, of course Matt had a checkup with his general physician on that morning.

Because the wedding was two hours from our home and because I needed to be at the wedding early for the photos, Matt's sister agreed to take him to the morning doctor's appointment and then he would ride to the wedding with my sister.

As I pulled into the church parking lot with my camera gear, I got a phone call.

Matt's doctor was sending him to a larger hospital. "I want to get some answers," Matt said. "We need to get to the bottom of this."

By this time, he was having not only abdominal pain but swelling in his midsection. The medical personnel planned to drain fluid from his belly and test it to determine what kind of infection he had.

As soon as I could, I extricated myself from the photo responsibilities thanks to my sister, who agreed to finish the shoot. (She's a professional photographer.)

Then I drove for three hours to the hospital.

My brother-in-law had reserved a room at the hospital's hospitality house where I could stay the night. I spent several hours with Matt that evening and then fell into bed at the house. The next morning I debated if I should check out before going to the hospital, but decided to wait.

I slept in that room for ten days.

In that time, Matt had fluid drawn from his belly four different times. The amount of fluid drawn was staggering and only relieved his tidal wave of pain for a short time.

The chemo doctor visited us on the second day we were there. The biopsy revealed that there was cancer in the lymph nodes now. He informed us that with this kind of cancer, the treatments on average extended life two years. He emphasized "on average" but we were riveted to the prognosis.

"How long do I have if I do nothing?" Matt asked.

The doctor drew in a breath. "Maybe two to three months. But please let me help you. I can help."

"I don't know if I want two years of torture. Maybe it'd be better to have two or three months of torture and be done," Matt said to me after the doctor left. "How do we decide?"

"Ultimately, you decide," I told him. I was sitting beside his bed and I held his hand. "But we will talk about it."

"We make good decisions together," he said. So we volleyed treatment options back and forth like two tennis players.

The next morning, he texted me. "I ordered breakfast." When I got to the room, there was a warm omelet waiting for me. "I'd be crazy not to do chemo," he said. "There are a few things I want to see. Write them down so I remember when the chemo gets bad."

I wrote them down.

Later in the day, he awoke from another pain-filled nap. "I think you'll be ok. You know how to live alone. And I'm okay with you remarrying. But promise me he'll be a believer."

My practical husband was working through details, as he always did. "I have no interest in remarrying," I said. "But I promise if God ever opens that door, he will be a faithful believer. I promise." This imaginary man would have to be incredibly special after my life with Matt.

Although I naively clung to the idea that Matt would soon turn the corner and come home so we could get chemo going, hindsight shows me he continued to decline day by day.

In the first few days at the hospital, he ordered me breakfast in the morning and called me at the hospitality house apartment at night to pray with me before we both went to sleep. After a few days, he wasn't able to answer his phone and certainly not text anymore. Or call. Or pray.

As his last week progressed, he struggled more and more with abdominal pain. One day, when he seemed fairly quiet, the nurse asked him what his pain level was.

"Seven."

Seven? I realized then that he'd been battling pain levels of eight and nine for days.

On Thursday, the medical staff seemed to get his pain level stabilized. Our daughter coaxed him to eat a little lunch - food had nauseated him for two days - and then he slept all afternoon.

In the evening, he woke up and scooted to the end of his bed. He swung his legs over the side. I sat an arm's length from his bed and I jumped up, wrapping my arms around him, afraid he'd fall.

"Where do you want to go?" I asked. He liked to sit in the recliner and I thought maybe that was his destination.

"I don't know. I need help. I need help. I don't know." He dropped his head on my shoulder as I wrapped my arms around him. His damp hair pressed against my cheek.

Those were his last words to me.

Hospital rules prohibited overnight stays, although I lingered as long as I could each day.

I returned to his room Friday morning expecting to see the upturn I'd been waiting for all week. Instead, several nurses clustered around his bed.

"He had a terrible night," one told me.

The Intensive Care Unit staff had spent time throughout the night stabilizing him. I asked a few questions and then the biggie: "Do I need to call the kids in to say goodbye?"

"Yes."

With Matt unconscious, I punched in a group text to our children: *I need to talk to you as soon as possible.*

Within an hour, I had spoken to all six of them, and they began rearranging plans. One daughter lived in Florida. She couldn't get a flight that day, but she was able to talk to her father on the phone. Amazingly, our oldest daughter, who lived in Canada, had already planned to fly in and would arrive at the hospital about 7 pm.

The day was a flurry of arrangements. Our children and their families gathered. One son and his wife have five young sons, ages twelve to four, and the hospital allowed them to come in to say goodbye. A daughter drove four hours with her family. The other children gathered as well.

Some dear friends stopped by. Matt's brother and his wife drove four hours to visit and his sister brought their 89-year-old mother for a final visit. Another brother called his farewell.

We discussed how to take shifts through the night so that Matt wasn't alone. Although the hospice nurse warned us that some people choose to die with no one present, I suspected he would go to eternity with loved ones holding his hands.

As the evening turned into night, we took turns reading scripture and praying. And grasping his hands as though we could keep him a little longer.

We read through several Psalms and then, shortly after midnight, one of our daughters asked if she could read Revelation 4 and 5. It describes the majesty of the throne room of God.

By the time she finished reading, Matt had entered that throne room.

Only ten weeks earlier, he spent an evening in the emergency room of our hospital wondering if he had a kidney stone. Now he was gone.

· · · · • · • · · · ·

I slept only a little the rest of that night. My head pounded like drums at a football game. My hands trembled and my muscles were like Jello. How could I go home to an empty house? I could think of so many things he'd planned to do. So many dreams we hadn't yet accomplished.

I went home. I allowed people to give me hugs, to cry with me, to bring meals, to help in innumerable ways.

Soon, when our back door opened, with that distinctive squeak we both knew so well, I expected to see him walk into the kitchen. I'm learning that *never* is a long time.

So how do I have hope when my partner is gone? We made a good team and now I do things alone. How do I go on?

In part by knowing that he has no more pain and no more cancer. By knowing he's being cared for and loved by Jesus forever. And I know I will see him again.

Those things comfort me.

And because of Matt's kindness and persistence in his faith walk, we both had many who now walk with me in love. Our church family prays. Matt was a talented drag racer and his racing family honors his faith and his influence. Our family offers many loving gestures.

These things honor Matt.

The day we were waiting for Matt to pass, a nurse told me, "Not all families could come together like this without tension. You're fortunate."

That, too, was a tribute to the life we had built together, a life that Matt had piloted.

But truly, I continue, day by day, largely because of the most important thing we shared: our faith in the Lord.

Again and again in this book I have tried to lay out the basic definition of hope: that what God has done in the past, he will do in the future. We can count on it.

Now I am living solo in our house. I think about what God did in the past. I remember Naomi's turnaround. Hannah's prayers. Daniel's faithfulness. I contemplate Bryan and Judy and Lydia and Leslie. They persevered despite disappointment and pain.

I recall how friends in pain - or facing terminal illness themselves - shout their praises to God because they trust in his presence every day, encouraging and comforting them.

God has done amazing things in the past and in the present. He rescues, he protects, he provides. That's his nature and he will continue doing those things.

Is God to blame for Matt's cancer, his pain, and his death? Matt and I discussed that question many times over the years when we observed other people enduring tragedies or hardships.

"God didn't do that," Matt told me. "We live in a broken world. Broken things happen."

Could God have healed Matt? He certainly has the power to do that, but is this world the best that God offers? It is not.

One day recently, I was feeling guilty because I am still alive, and Matt is gone. Then I realized he got the better deal. He doesn't worry about cancer anymore and he's in God's perfect place. He sees face to face what I try to see through faith.

This world is not our forever home. It's only a pothole-pocked highway on our way to the ultimate residence.

To eternity. Perfection. Comfort.

Ultimately, that is our hope. We hope for restoration in this world, but God has an even better future planned for us.

God has engineered the ultimate rescue. He asks us to hold on to his hand and glide into eternity. That's what faith is about.

Matt beat me to eternity, and I miss him desperately.

My heartbreak brings memories and tears in surprising waves of emotion. But I do not grieve without hope, for I know, as he knew, that he is spending eternity with Jesus.

I dare to hope.

· · · • • • • • · · ·

Digging Deeper

Do you have confidence that God has a greater plan for us than the things of this world? Explain what your confidence looks like.

After reading the stories in this book, do you confidently expect that God will rescue you? If not, check the appendix for suggestions on how to find that confidence, that hope.

Behind the Scenes

Matt Brasby died April 23, 2022 among those who loved him dearly. A Celebration of Life held a week later found our church overflowing with those who came to honor the faith and accomplishments of this man who served God with his whole heart.

As Jesus said: "I am the resurrection and the life. The one who believes in me will live, even though they die; and whoever lives by believing in me will never die." John 11:25

People continue to honor Matt's memory. His brother Paul began a Canada-to-Mexico bike trip a year ago, called The Great Divide. He made it to southern Wyoming before he had to return to work. Matt picked him up. They had planned the second half of the trip for the summer of 2022, with Matt returning him to the same spot in Wyoming so that Paul could continue the journey.

After Matt's death, Paul asked me to take him to Wyoming. I did, unaware that Paul had a special plan. He had printed a photo of himself and Matt riding bikes together several years ago. That photo was laminated to a small bag on the front of his bike.

"Matt's going with me on this trip," Paul said. And he then asked me to attach the bag to his bike. What an incredible honor to Matt's memory—and I was blessed to help. I think there may be more of those special tributes and they help me manage as well.

So, I continue day by day. The process of healing is uneven and unexpected, but I am committed to recovery.

* Mixed Martial Arts
** In the Colorado Rocky Mountains are a number of peaks that clear 14,000 feet. They are known as Colorado 14ers.

Appendix I: The Scroll

Those who do not remember the past are condemned to repeat it."
—George Santana
"But then I recall all you have done, O Lord; I remember your wonderful deeds of long ago."
—Psalm 77:11

・・・・●・●・・・

Today, we're not always encouraged to think of the past. A popular quote from Bill Keane says, "Yesterday's the past, tomorrow's the future, but today is a gift. That's why it's called the present." We make memes out of the idea of living in the now.

"Don't live in the past," we're warned. We don't want to get trapped by memories which might keep us from living today or make plans for tomorrow. And that's all good.

But there is value in learning from the past.

In the Introduction, I discussed muscle memory. Stories from the past—even recent past—help us develop a sort of muscle memory so we flex like a weight lifter when hardships hit us. We're more than ready.

The idea of remembering is common throughout the Bible. God often told his family to remember what he had done. Why? Because when we forget, we lose the value of the lesson.

Travel with me to the past to listen in on two young men living in Persia after the Exile (approximately 500 years before Jesus walked the earth), working to preserve the memories of God's chosen people, the Israelites. The Jews have honored the memories of their heritage for centuries and their commitment to preserving their history is valuable to them—and to us as Christians.

Some Christians may be hazy about the history of God's people in the Old Testament. I hope this story serves as a refresher.

Remembering what God has done in the past gives us the foundation of hope.

・・・●・●●・・・

Javad dipped his quill into the ink and scratched more words on the parchment, the ink flowing in bold black marks. His concentration was so deep that he didn't hear his friend Hosa enter the room.

"So you're doing it then?" Hosa stood across from Javad and put both hands on the large wooden table.

"I want to write it down. And my father asked me to do this."

Hosa nodded and then slung his leg over a wooden chair. "Not many write the stories down. We just tell them. Are you sure you can handle this?"

Javad poked the quill into the ink. "That's why I invited you. You know the stories better than I do."

"I should. The son of a rabbi, the line of Levi. Clear back to Aaron. I should know, and I'll be watching you." Hosa grinned. Maybe even winked. Then he looked around the small room. Stone walls. Slits for windows, letting in some hot air from the courtyard. Dancing orange torches attached to the wall. "Got anything to eat?"

Javad sighed. "I should have guessed. Are you always hungry?"

"Just here. You have the best fresh fruit."

Javad signaled to a servant. "Bring my friend refreshments."

"Clean food for me," Hosa said to the servant and then turned his attention to Javad. "You might be Yahweh-fearing, but you're still a Gentile."

"We eat like you now. Our entire household." Javad dropped the quill onto the table and blotted his last entry. A phantom butterfly flitted through his belly as he turned his project over to an expert. "Examine at my scroll. I've almost finished it, but there might be corrections."

"What if there are? Because I'm pretty sure I'll find something." A torch tossed shadows onto Hosa's face, but his teeth were bright.

Javad shrugged. "I'll re-write it. I want it perfect for Father." He handed the scroll to Hosa. "So read and tell me."

Hosa straightened his shoulders as he gripped the scroll and cleared his throat. Trying to appear important. He unrolled some of the parchment. "I will read it out loud. Don't argue," he said as Javad leaned in, preparing to do just that. "I will catch the mistakes if I can hear them. That's how I learned it."

"This could take all day." Javad rose from his chair and began pacing.

"Got anything better to do?" Hosa scanned the text and Javad walked, his muscles tight. "First, this is the story of the nation of Israel. Israelites. Not Jacobites."

"I didn't know for sure." Javad handed the quill to Hosa. "Mark out the word and change it."

"Can't you remember the correction?"

"Not like you can. I didn't grow up with these stories. I've only heard them after we became God-fearing."

Hosa nodded. "Just listen. It's our way and we preserve the stories as we tell them. It's your way now."

"I guess I'll have to learn."

"Plus, I don't want to write the corrections. Too messy." He glared at Javad, who wanted to protest again. Javad thought better of the complaint. He stood and began walking from wall to wall of the room. His servant stood at the door and stepped forward, expecting a command, but Javad waved him off. He needed to pace.

> "'*The*—'" Hosa paused his reading to correct the name. "'*—Israelites were of the family of Abraham, whom Yahweh sent to a new land. Abraham didn't know where Yahweh was sending him, but Yahweh made promises to Abraham.*

Hosa looked up. "You could add, '*Promises that Yahweh would bless him and his descendants, even though he didn't even have a son yet. And that Yahweh would never leave him and Yahweh would bless the nations through Abraham.*'"

Javad nodded, not willing to suggest again that Hosa write the addition. He would repeat Hosa's words until he could make notes. He would remember. Somehow, he could perk up his Persian brain for this new challenge. "Good promises."

Hosa continued reading,

> '*Abraham had a son, Isaac, And Isaac had two sons, Esau and Jacob. It was through Jacob that the family of Abraham continued. God's promise extended to Jacob's family.*'

Hosa nodded. "That works. There are a lot more details, of course, but you want a summary, right?"

"Right."

"Okay, let me read on—"

'Jacob had twelve sons.'

"Obviously that's important," Hosa said. "Good detail."

'The older brothers hated Joseph, Jacob's favorite son. And they sold him to slave traders going to Egypt. Joseph served as a slave and eventually ended up in prison in Egypt.'

Hosa stopped, his dark eyebrows furrowed. "Do you want to explain why he ended up in prison?"

Javad looked over his shoulder at Hosa and stopped walking before he met the wall in his pacing. "Do you think it's necessary in a summary? I can't include every detail."

Hosa twisted his mouth in thought. "Maybe not. It might be nice to add that it was an unfair accusation. But let me go on."

'Then Joseph became a ruler in Egypt.'

"Whoa, Javad, this isn't enough. You need to talk about his dreams. How Yahweh helped him interpret dreams. And about the Pharaoh's dream that predicted the years of plenty and years of famine."

"That's a lot of detail." This historical summary was going to be a lot longer than he had expected. A lot of re-writing for Javad while Hosa went home.

"Well, up to you," Hosa said. "But the dreams explain a lot. Let me read on."

> *'There was a famine that affected even Canaan, where Joseph's family had stayed. The brothers came to Egypt to buy food and there they met Joseph. He helped them to move to Egypt where they lived, protected by the Pharaoh for many years.'*

"Phew, I wish you had more details in the story."

"You haven't even gotten to Moses yet," Javad said. "It's an enormous story, this story of our ancestors."

"It is a massive story. And there is so much more, too. I heard Ezra is pulling together the official records, so maybe this is enough for—Well, what is this for?"

"For the rabbis to use when they teach their classes. Or for people who have forgotten the history. Maybe for Gentiles—"

"Gentiles? Are you serious? Why would they care?" Hosa glanced up at the servant. "Bring me water, please." The servant stepped away.

"Abraham's promise was for the nations. I mean, my family cares. I just thought—"

Hosa unrolled more of the scroll and waved his hand, shooing away Javad's concerns like flies. "No matter. Let me read."

> *'The family of Jacob was in Egypt for 400 years. In that time, the Egyptians forgot why*

they had come and instead made slaves of Jacob's family. The Egyptians badly oppressed them and they cried out to God.'

Hosa peeked over the top of the scroll. "I wish you could include more about Egyptians trying to kill the Israelite baby boys." He waved a hand in the air. "But I understand. Could you tell how Jacob's family had grown into a nation?" He sighed. "I know, a summary." He found his place in the text.

'Yahweh heard their cries for help and he sent Moses to rescue them.'

"I like that, Javad. *'Yahweh heard their cries for help.'* Yes."

"Thank you." Javad looked at his worktable, where the servants had stacked more parchment, ready for his writing. They'd obviously listened enough to know he'd have work to do after Hosa finished. A torch cast thin yellow light across the work. He'd be writing into the evening.

Hosa continued reading.

'Moses came to the Pharaoh to ask for the release of the Israelites. Pharaoh refused, believing he was stronger than the Israelites.'

Hosa lifted his head again. "Javad, you need to add that the Pharaoh thought he was a Yahweh, and he had a whole stable of other gods to help him. He wasn't afraid of Moses and this new god, even though we know how powerful Yahweh is."

"Yes." Javad had forgotten all those Egyptian gods because they had no strength. Like his former household gods, which also had no power. His father had loaded those little statues into a cart and had them smashed them to bits. Why would anyone trust them? None of those gods had protected themselves.

Hosa studied the scroll. He'd lost his place again. "I will continue."

> *'Moses faced the Pharaoh and Yahweh brought ten plagues, including the final one in which the angel of death killed the first-born son. But Yahweh provided a way for the Israelites to protect their first-born through a new ritual called the Passover. After the final plague, Pharaoh let the Israelites leave Egypt.'*

Hosa stopped reading and looked up.

Javad kept his eyes on Hosa's face. "You want more details about the plagues." Hosa had a theme that he could expect.

"I was thinking more details about the Passover. It is still such an important festival for us. How Yahweh provided a substitute—a lamb—for the first-born."

Javad nodded. "I need to do more research. I don't understand all the details of the Passover. And not all the details of the other plagues, either."

"This is a summary." Hosa was switching sides?

"A summary." A lame answer, but no sense in jostling Hosa's new position. Javad was happy to go along with Hosa.

Hosa searched the scroll quickly. "I'll read more.

> *'When the Israelites left Egypt, the Pharaoh changed his mind and pursued them. Yahweh opened the Red Sea in front of the people so they could pass through on dry land and then closed the Red Sea to destroy the Egyptians. Then the Israelites traveled through the wilderness to Mount Sinai, where Moses received Yahweh's laws.'*

Hosa placed the scroll on Javad's table. "Oh, good." The servant had laid a pitcher of water and a plate of cheese and fruit beside Hosa. He poured water into a cup. "My throat is parched."

"Take some fruit, too. For your strength. You must be utterly exhausted. From all the reading, I mean."

"Just trying to enjoy your barely adequate hospitality." Hosa grinned again and then drained his cup water, popped a grape into his mouth, and wiped his mouth. "My strength is restored, praise Yahweh." He drew a deep breath. "I can read more. Where was I? This is quite a gift I give you, my friend. My vast expertise."

"And my eternal gratitude. Get back to work."

Hosa studied the parchment. "Good fruit. We don't get that in our part of the city."

Javad shrugged. "So visit more often."

"I will. Where was I? Oh, here, with Moses on Mount Sinai."

> *'Then Yahweh told Moses how to build the Tabernacle, where Yahweh would live among his people. Yahweh had promised Abraham that Abraham's descendants would be his family.'*

Javad rubbed his hands together. "I didn't include a phrase, Hosa, but I remember it, where Yahweh tells his children, *'I will be your God and you will be my people.'* I wasn't sure if I should include it in a summary. Ezra will include it, I am sure."

Hosa nodded. "It's important to the story. Add it."

This re-write would take a while. Hosa's additions were going to make it twice as long. But maybe it was a good thing to include more details. As long as his hand didn't cramp from the writing.

Hosa refocused on the scroll and read,

> *'Our people call this event the Exile, where Yahweh rescued the Israelites from slavery and oppression. He used a rescuer who set them free. And then Yahweh brought them to the land he had promised them.'*

Hosa nodded. "I think that works. I want more detail, like about the spies and the 40 years in the wilderness. Those Israelites were foolish to doubt that Yahweh was strong enough to give them the land he promised. Why didn't they learn from our father, Abraham?" He sighed.

"Learn what?"

"You got this far and you have to ask?"

"I wrote Yahweh promised that Abraham would have many descendants, and it happened. More than that?"

"More. Like the birth of Isaac to two old people. Sarah was too old to have a baby, but yet, along came Isaac."

"I guess that would be considered impossible," Javad said.

"The Israelites must have forgotten about what Yahweh did with their ancestors. It's a good thing their children believed, or we'd never have gotten to the Promised Land."

Javad flicked at a fly wandering across the table. No pests should touch his parchments. "I suppose Ezra will include more details."

"I'm sure he will." Hosa lifted the scroll and read,

> *'The Israelites conquered many inhabitants of Canaan - the land Yahweh had promised them - through Joshua's leadership and Yahweh's strength. They settled in this land with each tribe getting a portion of the land.'*

"OK, Javad, you need to explain that the twelve brothers of Jacob became twelve tribes or clans. There are more details there, too."

"Of course." Javad grimaced. More writing. Hosa was the king of details. Javad's father wouldn't be getting this scroll as soon as Javad had thought.

"Did you include that horrible time during the time of the Judges? When the people didn't want Yahweh as their king after all he'd done?"

"Not really. I didn't want to include all that craziness. Father plans to read this to his grandchildren. He doesn't want to scare them."

Hosa nodded. "Maybe you can do a child-friendly version because, during that time, our people learned we needed a king. We don't do so well when we do whatever we want."

He cleared his throat again and began reading.

> *'David was the best king of Israel, a man after God's own heart. He ruled well, but his son, Solomon, worshipped many false gods.'*

Hosa looked up. "Javad, you need to talk more about false gods since Yahweh spoke against idolatry so many times."

"More?" Javad thought of the stories he had heard and not included. Stories of Israel joining in with their neighbors in worshipping other idols, just in case Yahweh wasn't strong enough. Maybe he hadn't included enough about the dangers of idolatry. About how Yahweh wanted loyalty to him only.

"Just think about it," Hosa said. He found his place to read again.

> *'After Solomon, Israel split into two nations. The northern ten tribes kept the name Israel, while the two southern tribes were called Judah. David's line continued through Judah's kings, but not Israel. The king of Israel taught his people to worship false idols.'*

Hosa nodded. "That bit about false idols is very important."

"My father crushed ours. The neighbors were angry, but the gods did nothing."

"How could they?" Hosa scanned the scroll. "Let me read on. I'm sure the Exile must be coming."

Javad settled back into his chair and drank from his cup. "The other E, huh? Exodus, where Yahweh brought his people out of slavery. And Exile, where they were sent back to slavery because they kept worshipping false gods."

"Like bookends," Hosa said. "My father can remember some of the Exile. It was a hard time."

Babylonians. Javad's teeth ground together. His people's enemies, but the Persians had conquered them.

Hosa read again,

> *'The Babylonians carried the Israelites away from the Promised Land. Yahweh gave my forefathers that land. The Babylonians de-*

> *stroyed Jerusalem and leveled the Temple in Jerusalem. My people believed Yahweh lived in the Temple.'*

"Good thing he didn't live just there or my family wouldn't be giving you fruit and cheese," Javad said.

"Maybe some sweet bread, too?"

"Forget it." Javad plucked a chunk of cheese from Hosa's plate and tossed it in his mouth.

Hosa sighed. "We learned that he didn't live only in Jerusalem. He's here, too."

"I agree. Even if it means feeding you."

Hosa gently tapped the scroll, which he had placed on the table again.

> *'The Israelites had to learn that Yahweh was with us and that he was more powerful than all those other gods.'*

"Gods which didn't exist, anyway. And had no power. And couldn't travel." Javad held out his hands as though he had won an argument.

"That's what *not existing* implies," Hosa said. "Just thinking about all this makes me want to go to synagogue and worship."

"Please finish my scroll first," Javad said. So Hosa unrolled the scroll further and scanned the last lines.

"Better than I expected. Make the corrections I suggested and let your father read it to your family." He handed the scroll back to Javad. "I'm curious. What have you learned through this project?"

"We were all hopeless—Jew and Gentile—but Yahweh handled it all. He never abandoned humans." Javad touched the scroll with the tip of his index finger. He would work on it soon, before he forgot the details Hosa had told him. "Thanks for helping me."

"You owe me a feast," Hosa said. "Bring the scroll to synagogue when you finish it. Maybe the rabbi will read it. It reminds us of who Yahweh is."

"A feast?"

"A big one." Hosa rose. "Keep writing, Javad. And keep remembering."

․․•••••••

Digging deeper
How familiar are you with the stories of God's people in the Old Testament? Knowing what God did in the past with his chosen people can help us understand more about God and his plans. What are some of those ways?

Read Acts 7:2-50. In that passage, Stephen summarizes Jewish history as he stands before the Jewish religious council. How did his report help you understand some of God's work in the Old Testament?

Behind the scenes

Hope anticipates the future based on the past. I included this fictional account to review what God did with the Israelites, as described in Old Testament history.

The Exodus and the Exile are key to understanding God's work. In both, we learn of God's desire to rescue and restore.

The history of God's expectations in the past helps us remember God wants us to reject other methods of caring for our wants and needs. The ancient ones trusted in idols and false gods. We have other ways to get what we want, but the motivation is still the same: trusting some force other than God for our desires.

Appendix II: Bible Verses About Hope

If you would like to go deeper into the hope exhibited by the people in the stories of this book, here are some verses to consider.

I'd suggest you read one passage and write what you've observed about hope. Yes, there are quite a few passages listed here but don't feel you have to reference them all. Start somewhere and read a little. You might find that looking at these is a little like eating potato chips: you bite into one and you want to try another.

Let God guide you in this study, if you choose to nibble on a few verses.

••••••••••

Job 11:18

Psalm 25:5

Psalm 31:24

Psalm 33:20

Psalm 62:5

Psalm 78:7

Psalm 119:114

Psalm 130:7

Psalm 62:5

Jeremiah 17:7

Jeremiah 29:11

APPENDIX II: BIBLE VERSES ABOUT HOPE

Romans 5:4-5

Romans 8:23

Romans 12:12

Romans 15:13

1 Corinthians 13:7

1 Corinthians 13:13

Ephesians 1:18

Ephesians 4:4

2 Thessalonians 2:16

1 Timothy 4:10

Titus 2:13

Hebrews 3:6

Hebrews 6:18-19

Hebrews 10:23

Hebrews 11:1

1 Peter 1:21

1 Peter 3:15

About the Author

Kathy Brasby's most annoying but maybe endearing trait is her intense curiosity. "Why" questions are the realm of 3-year-olds - and Kathy. Kathy is an award-winning writer, a former journalist, a blogger, a teacher, and a photographer who lives on a small hobby farm in northeast Colorado. She has six adult children and ten grandchildren.

Kathy earned a Masters of Theological Studies while her youngest children were still teenagers because, well, she has trouble turning down something new to learn. (Don't be waving more Internet classes front of her. She's booked for the next two years. At least)

She uses the information she gained in her Masters program to create many Bible study curriculums for classes she teaches, and to write some of the background material for the stories in this book.

Her wit appears in her blog posts, many of which are a comical recounting of that which happens when you have a family plus a farm. Plus friends and businesses. The material is endless.

Kathy's blog can be found at kathybrasby.net. She's also on Facebook, Instagram, and Twitter. Sometimes.